S0-AWA-673

SCIENCE

Everyday Science

TEACHER'S GUIDE & ASSESSMENTS

Lesson Notes

Activity Masters

Teacher Resources

PROPERTY OF
SILVERTON SCHOOL DIST. #1
SILVERTON, COLORADO

Reading Expeditions
Program Reviewers

Sylvia Roe Bath
Teacher
Lake Zurich CUSD 95
Lake Zurich, Illinois

Larry Bottjen
Reading Specialist
Matanuska-Susitna Borough
  School District
Palmer, Alaska

Bonnie Goodrich
Learning Specialist
Plymouth-Canton Community
  Schools
Canton, Michigan

Karen Gardner Lantz
Curriculum Specialist
Plano Independent School
  District
Plano, Texas

Cheryl Larison
Teacher
Alisal Union School District
Salinas, California

Joanne C. Letwinch
Teacher
Haddonfield Public Schools
Haddonfield, New Jersey

Joan C. Radford
Principal
Hopkins County Schools
Madisonville, Kentucky

Kirk Robbins
Teacher
Renton School District
Renton, Washington

Randall C. Stom
Science Specialist
Green Acres School
Rockville, Maryland

May Tilghman
Coordinating Literacy Teacher
Wake County Public Schools
Raleigh, North Carolina

Alie Victorine
Teacher
Franklin-McKinley School District
San Jose, California

Stephani Wise
Teacher
Richardson Independent
  School District
Richardson, Texas

Reading Expeditions
Consultants

For Second Language Learners
Illinois Resource Center
Des Plaines, Illinois

For Gifted and Talented Students
Cheryl Saltzman
Former Program Director
Wisconsin Center for
  Academically Talented Youth
Madison, Wisconsin

For Children with Special Needs
Julie Hoban Morrison
Special Needs Teacher
Dedham, Massachusetts

Copyright © 2004 National Geographic Society

All rights reserved. Reproduction of the whole or any part of the contents without written permission from the publisher is prohibited. National Geographic, National Geographic School Publishing, and the Yellow Border are registered trademarks of the National Geographic Society.

The purchasing educational institution and its staff are permitted to make copies of the pages marked as activity master pages. These pages may be photocopied for non-commercial classroom use only.

Published by the National Geographic Society, Washington, D.C. 20036

ISBN: 0-7922-4858-9
Product # 42048

Produced through the worldwide resources of the National Geographic Society, John M. Fahey, Jr., President and Chief Executive Officer; Gilbert M. Grosvenor, Chairman of the Board; Nina D. Hoffman, Executive Vice President and President, Books and Education Publishing Group.

PREPARED BY NATIONAL GEOGRAPHIC SCHOOL PUBLISHING
Ericka Markman, Senior Vice President and President, Children's Books and Education Publishing Group; Steve Mico, Vice President, Editorial Director; Rosemary Baker, Executive Editor; Barbara Seeber, Editorial Manager; Jim Hiscott, Design Manager; Kristin Hanneman, Illustrations Manager; Matt Wascavage, Manager of Publishing Services; Sean Philpotts, Production Manager; Jane Ponton, Production Artist.

Manufacturing and Quality Control
Christopher A. Liedel, Chief Financial Officer; Phillip L. Schlosser, Director; Clifton M. Brown, Manager

Editorial Services: The Mazer Corporation, Creative Services Associates, Inc.
Writers: Leslie Morrison and Erin Cleary

Editor: Amy Sarver
Teacher's Guide Design: Steven Curtis Design, Inc.

Picture Credits for the Teacher's Guide:
Cover: background, Robert Finken/Index Stock Imagery/PictureQuest; photos (top to bottom): PhotoDisc®; Digital Vision; book covers, top row (left to right): Stacy D. Gold, National Geographic Image Collection; Georgette Douwma, Getty Images; Massis J. Boujikian/Corbis; PhotoDisc® (3); Digital Stock (2); Digital Vision (4); Corbis; PhotoDisc® (3); Kenneth M. Highfill/Photo Researchers; Stephen Simpson, Getty Images; Meckes/Ottawa/ Eye of Science/Photo Researchers; Digital Stock; Stockbyte; bottom row (left to right): Terry W. Eggers/Corbis, middle, Chris carroll/Corbis, (bottom left) LWA-Sharie Kennedy/Corbis, (bottom middle) Bananastock, Groups, Kids, & Teenagers/Creatas; Photodisc, Shopping List/Creatas; cover insets (middle left) Rubberball, Silhouettes of Occupations/Creatas, (bottom left), Yoshio Tomii/SuperStock, (bottom right) Myrleen Ferguson Cate/PhotoEdit; ©Chris Daniels/Corbis; Cover instes (top left) © Jose Luis Pelaez, Inc./Corbis, (middle) © Mazer Corporation, (bottom middle) © Creatas; Cover background: Ralph Krubner/Index Stock Imagery; cover insets (top right) PhotoDisc/Everyday Objects, (middle right) PhotoDisc/Just Documents, (bottom right) PhotoDisc/The Signature Series/Everyday People, (bottom middle), Francisco Cruz/SuperStock, (bottom left) PhotoDisc, (middle left) The Mazer Corporation; Cover background, Owaki-Kulla/Corbis; cover insets (bottom left), Johnny Johnson/Animals Animals, (middle right) Imagesource, Travel Icons/Creatas, (bottom right) Digital Vision, Life Underwater/Creatas, (bottom middle) Digital Vision, Life Underwater/ Creatas, (bottom middle) Digital Vision, Life Underwater/Creatas; Back cover: Digital Vision. Page 1: Digital Stock.

Line art by Creative Services Associates, Inc.

Contents

Lesson Notes

More Science of You 10
Science Around the House 18
Science at the Airport 26
Science at the Aquarium 34
Science at the Grocery 42
Science at the Mall 50
Science at the Park 58
Science at the Sandy Shore 66
Science at the Zoo 74
The Science of You 82

Teacher Resources

Series Overview 4
Lesson Overview 6
Meeting Individual Needs 90
Overview of Titles and Skills 96
Correlation to National Standards 100
Literacy Internet Resources 102
Assessment Overview 104
Multiple-Choice Tests..106
Answer Key for Multiple-Choice Tests 116
Using Portfolios and Retellings 117
Using Graphic Organizers 121
Index 127

Series Overview

Introduction

The *Everyday Science* series explores basic science concepts in everyday life. In this series students learn that many everyday situations, such as going to the park, hanging around the house, or going to the grocery store, are filled with science and technology. The books present standards-based science content through carefully formatted texts designed to develop nonfiction reading skills. Photographs, captions, and illustrations support the text and help students navigate through each book.

The organization of this series taps into the natural curiosity of young readers. Instead of the typical chapter organization of many books, this series builds related concepts with each two-page spread. Each spread ends with a question or phrase that invites the reader to turn the page to find out more. This format keeps readers actively engaged as they build their comprehension of science concepts. While each book focuses on a topic, the science within each book follows standard science strands.

- *More Science of You:* life science and the human body
- *Science Around the House:* physical and life science
- *Science at the Airport:* physical science
- *Science at the Aquarium:* life science
- *Science at the Grocery:* life and physical science
- *Science at the Mall:* physical science
- *Science at the Park:* life science
- *Science at the Sandy Shore:* life and Earth science
- *Science at the Zoo:* life science
- *The Science of You:* life science and the human body

Focus on Literacy
Developing Comprehension Skills

The series is designed to help students develop and practice essential reading skills. Opportunities to develop specific comprehension skills are featured in the individual lesson notes for each title. The following skills are presented:

Identify facts and opinions
Make generalizations
Paraphrase
Identify main idea and details
Draw conclusions
Make judgments
Use context clues
Identify sequence of events
Summarize
Compare and contrast
Identify cause-and-effect relationships

Understanding Nonfiction Genres, Text Features, and Graphics

Successful readers of informational text are adept at reading various genres and formats. Being proficient at using the diverse characteristics of nonfiction texts is essential to understanding informational material. The following nonfiction features are incorporated in the *Everyday Science* series:

Genres
Expository

Text Features
Headings
Captions and labels

Parts of a Book
Contents page
Glossary

Graphic Information
Photographs
Illustrations

Reading Across Texts

Recent research in student reading behaviors and proficiency indicates students' reading skills are enhanced when they have opportunities to read and compare multiple texts. This series provides an excellent opportunity to read varied texts on the same general theme: Science is a part of our everyday lives. In comparing and contrasting multiple texts, students can evaluate content as well as text organization and presentation. Students might discuss the following questions:

> **Compare**—How are the books organized? How are book organizations alike and different?
> **Evaluate**—Is the information presented clearly? What features are helpful in understanding a topic?
> **Generalize**—What characteristics are shared by the topics of each book in the series? How are the topics different? How do they contribute to the overall understanding of science concepts?

Focus on Science
Developing Science Process Skills

Each *Everyday Science* title provides opportunities for students to develop science skills. The lessons in this teacher's guide provide students with opportunities to engage in scientific inquiry as they use scientific reasoning and critical thinking to develop their understanding. Each book in the *Everyday Science* series is paired with a science process skill that helps students as they develop their abilities to think in ways associated with scientific inquiry. The following process skills are highlighted in the *Everyday Science* series:

* Classifying—*Science at the Grocery, Science at the Sandy Shore*
* Creating a Bar Graph—*Science at the Aquarium, Science at the Zoo*
* Collecting Data—*The Science of You*
* Observing—*Science Around the House, Science at the Airport, Science at the Mall, Science at the Park*
* Reading a Graph—*More Science of You*

Core Concepts

This series encourages students to explore science in their everyday lives. By carefully examining a common setting, students learn fundamental science principles and realize how these principles influence everyday activities. The titles in the *Everyday Science* series provide students with the opportunity to read engaging nonfiction. Core concepts developed in the series support National Science Education Standards, including the following:

LIFE SCIENCE: Grades K–4
* Characteristics of organisms
* Life cycles of organisms
* Organisms and environments

PHYSICAL SCIENCE: Grades K–4
* Properties of objects and materials
* Position and motion of objects
* Light, heat, electricity, and magnetism

EARTH SCIENCE: Grades K–4
* Properties of Earth materials
* Changes in Earth and sky

SCIENCE AND TECHNOLOGY: Grades K–4
* Understanding about science and technology
* Abilities to distinguish between natural objects and objects made by humans

SCIENCE IN PERSONAL AND SOCIAL PERSPECTIVES: Grades K–4
* Personal health
* Science and technology in local challenges
* Changes in environments

HISTORY AND NATURE OF SCIENCE: Grades K–4
* Science as a human endeavor

SCIENCE AS INQUIRY: Grades K–4
* Abilities necessary to do scientific inquiry
* Understanding about scientific inquiry

Overview The Overview page saves time in selecting books and planning instruction.

Summary
A brief summary highlights the main ideas and important details of the book.

Science Background
Additional information about the places, the people, and the science topics related to the book provides a context for the book.

Learning Objectives
Key learning objectives in nonfiction features and genre, as well as reading, writing, and science process skills and strategies, are listed to make planning efficient.

Overview

More Science of You

By Kate Boehm Jerome

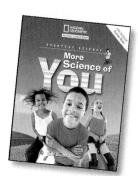

Summary

The book, *More Science of You*, is an extension of *The Science of You*. Among many interesting facts, students will learn how the skeletal system protects their internal organs, supports their body, and provides a place for muscles to attach. Questions ranging from why baby teeth are replaced by adult teeth to why humans sneeze, shiver, and yawn will be examined to provide insight into the incredible workings of the human body.

Science Background

The human body is an amazing machine made up of many parts. Learning about these parts and how they function is the focus of two broad areas of life science: anatomy and physiology. Anatomy is the branch of life science concerned with the study of the structures that make up living things. Physiology is the study of how the various structures (from individual cells to complete organ systems) of living things function to carry out the processes necessary for life.

Learning Objectives

Science	Process Skills	Reading Skills	Writing Skills
• Identify the functions of bones • Describe how fingernails grow • Explain the role of the tongue and the nose in taste • Explain why the body reacts to mosquito bites	**Skill Focus** • Reading a graph **Supporting Skills** • Observing • Collecting data	**Genre: Expository** **Skill Focus** • Make and check predictions • Determine word knowledge **Supporting Skills** • Identify main idea and details • Summarize	**Writing Focus** • Write a newspaper article (expository) **Supporting Skills** • Use the writing process • Conduct research **Speaking and Listening** • Give an oral presentation

10 *More Science of You*

Focus on Reading
Suggested activities help students develop strategies to use before, during, and after reading.

Focus on Reading

Before Reading

Activate Prior Knowledge

Have students review the contents page. Ask students to consider what they know about each topic listed. For example, write the word *bones* on the board and ask:

> *What are bones?*
>
> *What do bones do?*

Write students' ideas on a K-W-L chart on the board (see chart below). In the first column, write what students know about bones. In the second column, write questions they have about bones. In the third column, record what students have learned after reading the book.

Ask students to copy the K-W-L chart in their notebooks and work with a partner to complete the first two columns for each topic. Have students return to the chart after reading to identify what they have learned.

Preview

Give students time to flip through the book. Ask them to look at the pictures and pay close attention to the section titles. Ask:

> *What is this book about?*
>
> *What will you learn about the human body?*

Set Purpose

Ask students whether this book reminds them of other books they have read. Have them set a purpose for reading.

Vocabulary Strategy: Determine Word Knowledge
Activity Master, Page 14

Explain that the vocabulary words in the book are related to health and the body. Tell students that on the Activity Master on page 14, they will use the text and glossary of *More Science of You* to write a sentence that relates each vocabulary word to health or the human body. Students will use these words:

- allergies
- primary teeth
- saliva
- skeletal system
- taste buds

What I Know	What I Want to Know	What I Learned

Correlation to National Standards

Science	Reading/Language Arts	State/Local
• Scientific inquiry (K–4) • Characteristics of organisms (K–4) • Science as a human endeavor (K–4) • Life cycles of organisms (K–4) • Personal health (K–4)	• Read to be informed • Apply language structures and conventions • Use and adjust visual and written language to communicate effectively • Use information in text and prior experience to answer questions and verify information • Use the writing process	_____ _____ _____ _____

See Standards Chart on page 101.

More Science of You 11

Activate Prior Knowledge

Graphic aids are often used to help organize prior knowledge.

Preview

Previewing nonfiction text helps students to understand how the text is organized and to anticipate what kinds of information will be included.

Vocabulary Strategy

Students use an Activity Master to work with content words prior to reading.

Correlation to National Standards

Content is correlated to national standards to ensure that key concepts are covered. A chart correlating all titles to national standards is on page 101 of this book.

Focus on Reading
Suggested activities help students develop strategies to use before, during, and after reading.

Read Strategically
An Activity Master is provided to develop essential comprehension skills. The **Strategy Tip** offers concrete tips to help develop metacognitive strategies.

Meeting Individual Needs
Use the strategies starting on page 90 of this book to modify instruction to meet the needs of special learners.

Responding
Discussion questions help students to examine the main ideas included in each book.

Writing and Research
Students research topics and write in a variety of genres and forms.

Communicating
Activities help students develop the communication skills of listening, speaking, and viewing.

Focus on Reading (continued)

During Reading

Read Strategically: Make and Check Predictions
Activity Master, Page 15

Assign each section of the book as independent reading. As students read, they can use the Activity Master on page 15 to help them focus on the main ideas in *More Science of You*. Suggest that students use the questions that begin each topic to help them predict what they will learn on each set of pages. They should then check their prediction as they read each section. To model the process, make a prediction as a class and check it together after reading the first section.

Strategy Tip: Self-question
To help students check their own comprehension, suggest that they ask themselves questions about the topic they are reading. For example, they might ask:

Do I understand what each section of this book is mostly about?

After reading, can I answer the question asked at the beginning of each section?

For questions they cannot answer, students can reread sections of the book with those questions in mind. If students are still having difficulty, they can ask for clarification during the follow-up class discussion.

Meeting Individual Needs
For specific strategies on meeting individual needs, see pages 90–95.

After Reading

Responding
Initiate a class discussion to assess reading comprehension. Ask:

How do a baby's bones differ from an adult's bones? (See page 6 in the student book.) **(compare and contrast)**

How do fingernails grow? (See page 8.) **(sequence)**

What parts of the body help you taste your food? (See pages 10–11.) **(draw conclusions)**

What are ways the body can react to allergies? (See pages 12–13 and 14.) **(identify cause-and-effect relationships)**

What causes shivering? (See pages 16–17.) **(identify cause-and-effect relationships)**

What are primary teeth? (See pages 18–19.) **(summarize)**

What do you think causes yawning? (See pages 20–21.) **(make judgments)**

Writing and Research: Write a Newspaper Article
Activity Master, Page 16

Tell students they are going to write an article for their local newspaper. Their assignment is to answer the letter a young reader sent to the "Questions Kids Ask" column of the newspaper. Students can use *More Science of You*, the Internet, and library resources, such as science books or encyclopedias, as resources for their responses. The Activity Master on page 16 will help students organize their ideas.

Communicating: Speaking/Listening
Give an oral presentation
In small groups, students can read their articles.

Students reading should
✓ speak clearly
✓ make eye contact with listeners
✓ adapt speech as appropriate

Listeners should
✓ listen politely
✓ distinguish between speakers' opinions and facts
✓ ask questions to clarify ideas they didn't understand

Extend and Assess
A focus on science, assessment, and extension activities provides a variety of instructional options.

Extend and Assess

Focus on Science

Thinking Like a Scientist
Process Skill: Reading a Graph
Activity Master, Page 17
Explain to students that the graph on the Activity Master on page 17 shows the number of baby teeth that a student lost at different ages. Students will use the information given in the graph to answer the questions that follow.

Answers: 1 *Answers will vary but the title should be relevant to the chart.* **2** *The student lost the most teeth at age 9.* **3** *The student lost the fewest teeth at age 6.*

Life Science: Create a Body System Poster
Remind students that each body system has a specific purpose. Body systems are discussed in *More Science of You*. Have students prepare a poster showing at least one body system. They can draw pictures illustrating the system they chose or they can find pictures relating to the system in magazines. They should tell in a few words how each system is important. Have students give their posters a title.

Assessment Options
Use the following assessment options to assess students' understanding of *More Science of You*.

Questions
Use the following questions during individual conferences or ask students to write answers in their notebooks.

1 Why are bones important to the body?
2 What four kinds of taste can taste buds detect?
3 What is a reflex action?
4 What causes you to lose a primary tooth?
5 Why do people yawn?

Assessment Activity
Ask students to create an eight-page booklet titled *Interesting Facts About My Body*. Have students make one page in their booklets for each topic discussed in *More Science of You*. Each page should include one fact and one illustration.

Booklets should

✓ be well-organized and carefully prepared
✓ use both words and images to communicate ideas
✓ use correct grammar and mechanics

Multiple-Choice Test
Use the multiple-choice test on page 106.

Cross-Curricular Connection

Mathematics
Have students use the information about bones to calculate how many fewer bones are in the body of an adult than in a newborn.

Home-School Connection
Students can find a newspaper or magazine article that discusses a topic related to the human body. They can then discuss the main ideas from the article with parents and explain how the topics in the article relate to information in *More Science of You*.

More Science of You

Focus on Science
Activities developing key science concepts and skills help students understand the books in new ways. An Activity Master develops essential process skills.

Assessment
Use the discussion questions, the assessment activity, or the multiple-choice test to evaluate students' understanding of important concepts in the book.

Cross-Curricular Connection
Suggested activities provide opportunities to integrate science content with math, social studies, music, art, and literature.

Home-School Connection
Home-school connections offer ideas for students to talk about their work with family members.

More Science of You 13

More Science of You

By Kate Boehm Jerome

Summary

The book, *More Science of You,* is an extension of *The Science of You.* Among many interesting facts, students will learn how the skeletal system protects their internal organs, supports their body, and provides a place for muscles to attach. Questions ranging from why baby teeth are replaced by adult teeth to why humans sneeze, shiver, and yawn will be examined to provide insight into the incredible workings of the human body.

Science Background

The human body is an amazing machine made up of many parts. Learning about these parts and how they function is the focus of two broad areas of life science: anatomy and physiology. Anatomy is the branch of life science concerned with the study of the structures that make up living things. Physiology is the study of how the various structures (from individual cells to complete organ systems) of living things function to carry out the processes necessary for life.

Learning Objectives

Science

- Identify the functions of bones
- Describe how fingernails grow
- Explain the role of the tongue and the nose in taste
- Explain why the body reacts to mosquito bites

Process Skills

Skill Focus
- Reading a graph

Supporting Skills
- Observing
- Collecting data

Reading Skills

Genre: Expository

Skill Focus
- Make and check predictions
- Determine word knowledge

Supporting Skills
- Identify main idea and details
- Summarize

Writing Skills

Writing Focus
- Write a newspaper article (expository)

Supporting Skills
- Use the writing process
- Conduct research

Speaking and Listening
- Give an oral presentation

Focus on Reading

Before Reading

Activate Prior Knowledge

Have students review the contents page. Ask students to consider what they know about each topic listed. For example, write the word *bones* on the board and ask:

What are bones?

What do bones do?

Write students' ideas on a K-W-L chart on the board (see chart below). In the first column, write what students know about bones. In the second column, write questions they have about bones. In the third column, record what students have learned after reading the book.

Ask students to copy the K-W-L chart in their notebooks and work with a partner to complete the first two columns for each topic. Have students return to the chart after reading to identify what they have learned.

Preview

Give students time to flip through the book. Ask them to look at the pictures and pay close attention to the section titles. Ask:

What is this book about?

What will you learn about the human body?

Set Purpose

Ask students whether this book reminds them of other books they have read. Have them set a purpose for reading.

Vocabulary Strategy: Determine Word Knowledge

Activity Master, Page 14

Explain that the vocabulary words in the book are related to health and the body. Tell students that on the Activity Master on page 14, they will use the text and glossary of *More Science of You* to write a sentence that relates each vocabulary word to health or the human body. Students will use these words:

allergies
primary teeth
saliva
skeletal system
taste buds

What I Know	What I Want to Know	What I Learned

Correlation to National Standards

Science	Reading/Language Arts	State/Local
• Scientific inquiry (K–4) • Characteristics of organisms (K–4) • Science as a human endeavor (K–4) • Life cycles of organisms (K–4) • Personal health (K–4)	• Read to be informed • Apply language structures and conventions • Use and adjust visual and written language to communicate effectively • Use information in text and prior experience to answer questions and verify information • Use the writing process	_____ _____ _____ _____

See Standards Chart on page 101.

During Reading

Read Strategically: Make and Check Predictions

Activity Master, Page 15

Assign each section of the book as independent reading. As students read, they can use the Activity Master on page 15 to help them focus on the main ideas in *More Science of You*. Suggest that students use the questions that begin each topic to help them predict what they will learn on each set of pages. They should then check their prediction as they read each section. To model the process, make a prediction as a class and check it together after reading the first section.

Strategy Tip: Self-question

To help students check their own comprehension, suggest that they ask themselves questions about the topic they are reading. For example, they might ask:

Do I understand what each section of this book is mostly about?

After reading, can I answer the question asked at the beginning of each section?

For questions they cannot answer, students can reread sections of the book with those questions in mind. If students are still having difficulty, they can ask for clarification during the follow-up class discussion.

Meeting Individual Needs

For specific strategies on meeting individual needs, see pages 90–95.

After Reading

Responding

Initiate a class discussion to assess reading comprehension. Ask:

How do a baby's bones differ from an adult's bones? (See page 6 in the student book.) **(compare and contrast)**

How do fingernails grow? (See page 8.) **(sequence)**

What parts of the body help you taste your food? (See pages 10–11.) **(draw conclusions)**

What are ways the body can react to allergies? (See pages 12–13 and 14.) **(identify cause-and-effect relationships)**

What causes shivering? (See pages 16–17.) **(identify cause-and-effect relationships)**

What are primary teeth? (See pages 18–19.) **(summarize)**

What do you think causes yawning? (See pages 20–21.) **(make judgments)**

Writing and Research: Write a Newspaper Article

Activity Master, Page 16

Tell students they are going to write an article for their local newspaper. Their assignment is to answer the letter a young reader sent to the "Questions Kids Ask" column of the newspaper. Students can use *More Science of You*, the Internet, and library resources, such as science books or encyclopedias, as resources for their responses. The Activity Master on page 16 will help students organize their ideas.

Communicating: Speaking/Listening

Give an oral presentation

In small groups, students can read their articles.

Students reading should

✓ speak clearly
✓ make eye contact with listeners
✓ adapt speech as appropriate

Listeners should

✓ listen politely
✓ distinguish between speakers' opinions and facts
✓ ask questions to clarify ideas they didn't understand

Extend and Assess

Focus on Science

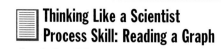

Thinking Like a Scientist
Process Skill: Reading a Graph

Activity Master, Page 17

Explain to students that the graph on the Activity Master on page 17 shows the number of baby teeth that a student lost at different ages. Students will use the information given in the graph to answer the questions that follow.

Answers: 1 *Answers will vary but the title should be relevant to the chart.* **2** *The student lost the most teeth at age 9.* **3** *The student lost the fewest teeth at age 6.*

Life Science: Create a Body System Poster

Remind students that each body system has a specific purpose. Body systems are discussed in *More Science of You*. Have students prepare a poster showing at least one body system. They can draw pictures illustrating the system they chose or they can find pictures relating to the system in magazines. They should tell in a few words how each system is important. Have students give their posters a title.

Assessment Options

Use the following assessment options to assess students' understanding of *More Science of You*.

Questions

Use the following questions during individual conferences or ask students to write answers in their notebooks.

1 Why are bones important to the body?

2 What four kinds of taste can taste buds detect?

3 What is a reflex action?

4 What causes you to lose a primary tooth?

5 Why do people yawn?

Assessment Activity

Ask students to create an eight-page booklet titled *Interesting Facts About My Body*. Have students make one page in their booklets for each topic discussed in *More Science of You*. Each page should include one fact and one illustration.

Booklets should

✓ be well-organized and carefully prepared

✓ use both words and images to communicate ideas

✓ use correct grammar and mechanics

Multiple-Choice Test

Use the multiple-choice test on page 106.

Cross-Curricular Connection

Mathematics

Have students use the information about bones to calculate how many fewer bones are in the body of an adult than in a newborn.

Home-School Connection

Students can find a newspaper or magazine article that discusses a topic related to the human body. They can then discuss the main ideas from the article with parents and explain how the topics in the article relate to information in *More Science of You*.

Vocabulary: Determine Word Knowledge

Each word or term below is related to your health or your body in some way.
In the first column, write what you already know about each word. Then use
More Science of You and its glossary to find new information about each word.
Write a sentence that relates each word to your health or your body.

Word	What I Already Know	My Sentence About Health/Body
allergies		
primary teeth		
saliva		
skeletal system		
taste buds		

Reading: Make and Check Predictions

As you read *More Science of You,* predict what each section will be about. Write your prediction as a sentence that states what you think you will learn about each topic in the chart. Then continue reading to see how close your prediction was. In the "Check" column of the chart, explain how close your prediction was and add information that was different from what you predicted.

Section	Prediction	Check
Skeletal System		
Fingernails		
The Sense of Taste		
Mosquito Bites		
Allergies		
Shivering		
Baby Teeth		
Yawning		

Writing: Write an Article

You are the writer of the "Questions Kids Ask" section of your local newspaper. You need to write an article to answer the questions in the letter shown below. To research and write your article, you can use *More Science of You,* the Internet, or books or encyclopedias found in the library. Use the space below to organize your ideas.

Dear Questions Kids Ask:

I love to swim. Sometimes, when I get out of the pool I get cold. When this happens, I shiver. Soon, my arms and legs are covered with little bumps. What are these bumps and what causes them? Are they harmful?

Sally

---

1. Identify the question or questions you need to answer in your article.

   _____

   _____

2. Briefly describe the information your article must include to answer the reader.

   _____

   _____

3. List any other ideas you would like to include.

   _____

   _____

4. Photos and other images can help explain ideas. What photo or image would you like to include with your article?

   _____

   _____

Thinking Like a Scientist: Reading a Graph

Many people begin losing their teeth at the age of six or seven. The graph below shows the number of teeth that one student lost at different ages. Read the information shown on the graph and answer the questions below.

Title: _____

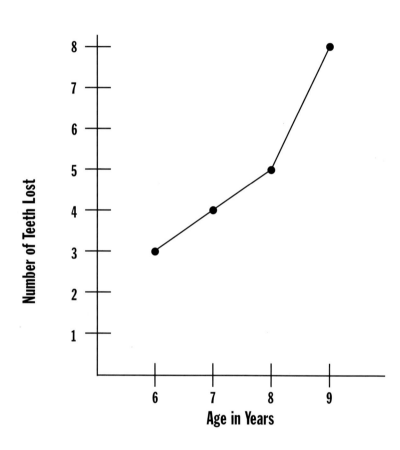

Use the graph to answer the following questions.

1. What is a good title for your graph? Write it on the line provided above the graph.

2. At what age did the student lose most of her teeth? _____

3. At what age shown on the chart did she lose the fewest teeth? _____

© 2004 National Geographic Society

Science Around the House

By Kate Boehm Jerome
and Vince Sipkovich

Summary

The average home is filled with science and technology. But because household objects and devices are so familiar, we often do not recognize the learning opportunities they present. *Science Around the House* discusses many different items or situations in the average home and gives a scientific basis for them. The book begins on the floor, offering a look at tiny dust mites and explaining how a vacuum cleaner works to pick them up. In the bathroom, the science of sound and vibration is introduced. In the kitchen, readers learn about the science of microwaves, soda pop, and soap bubbles.

Science Background

The study of science is not confined to the classroom. Students can see examples of science in every room of their homes. *Science Around the House* helps students understand how science affects their lives during everyday activities. This book also provides explanations and answers questions that students may have about the science in their homes, such as how smoke detectors work and how a remote control changes channels on the television.

Learning Objectives

Science

- Explain how dust can trigger an allergy
- Identify examples of technology in the home
- Explain how sound travels
- Understand that science helps answer questions about the world

Process Skills

Skill Focus
- Observing

Supporting Skills
- Inferring
- Communicating

Reading Skills

Genre: Expository
Skill Focus
- Identify cause-and-effect relationships
- Determine word knowledge

Supporting Skills
- Draw conclusions
- Make generalizations
- Summarize

Writing Skills

Writing Focus
- Write a list of facts (expository)

Supporting Skills
- Prewrite
- Conduct research

Speaking and Listening
- Read a list of facts aloud

Focus on Reading

Before Reading

Activate Prior Knowledge

Conduct an informal survey to find out how many students have used a microwave oven. Have them explain how they use it and discuss how they think it works. Guide students to understand that there is a scientific process involved. Explain that the book they are about to read explains how science is used to make other things happen in their homes as well. Mention some of the other topics covered in the book and have students write a list of what they would like to know about each one. (See the sample below.)

Preview

Give students time to look through the book, paying attention to headings, photos, and captions. Ask:

After looking at the photographs, what are some processes that you think this book will discuss?

What additional information can be found in the captions?

What machines will we be reading about in this book?

Set Purpose

Ask students whether this book reminds them of other books they have read. Have them set a purpose for reading. Ask:

What do you think you can learn by reading this book?

Encourage students to give reasons for their answers.

Vocabulary Strategy: Determine Word Knowledge

Activity Master, Page 22

Turn to page 6 and point out the word *microscope*. Ask students what they know about this word, and write their ideas on the board. Relate the word to science. Explain that students will work with other words that pertain to science around the house. On the Activity Master on page 22, have students write a definition for each word. Then, as they read, they can write a sentence that relates each word to the topic of science around the house. Students will use the following vocabulary words:

allergic
filter
microwaves
smoke detector
sound
steam

Topic	What I Would Like to Know
television remote control	How does it work? Do I have to point it directly at the television set to make it work?

Correlation to National Standards

Science	Reading/Language Arts	State/Local
• Properties of objects and materials (K–4) • Position and motion of objects (K–4) • Science and technology (K–4) • Personal health (K–4)	• Read to build an understanding of applications of science in a home • Apply a wide range of strategies to comprehend and interpret texts • Use the writing process • Conduct research • Use written and oral language to communicate • Use a variety of informational resources	_____ _____ _____ _____ **See Standards Chart on page 101.**

During Reading

 Read Strategically: Identify Cause-and-Effect Relationships

Activity Master, Page 23

Assign each two-page spread of the book as independent reading. As students read, they can use the Activity Master on page 23 to write causes and effects related to science around the house.

Remind students that an effect is what happens and a cause is why it happens. Identifying causes and effects can help students see connections between events.

Strategy Tip: Summarize

Suggest to students that they summarize paragraphs they have difficulty understanding. When they summarize, they have to think through the main ideas of the paragraph so that they can present them briefly and accurately. If students have difficulty summarizing a paragraph, they should take a few moments to figure out unfamiliar words and examine confusing sentence structure.

Meeting Individual Needs

For specific strategies on meeting individual needs, see pages 90–95.

After Reading

Responding

Initiate a class discussion to assess reading comprehension. Ask:

Choose a machine discussed in the student book and describe it. Tell how its parts help it do the things it does. (See pages 8, 10, 14, and 20 in the student book.) **(summarize)**

What effect do small spaces have on how sound travels? (See page 12.) **(identify cause-and-effect relationships)**

Complete this statement: "Most of the tools in this book . . ." (See pages 8, 10, 14, 18, and 20.) **(make generalizations)**

What conclusion can you draw about how microwaves have improved cooking? (See pages 14–15.) **(draw conclusions)**

Which of the tools described in this book did you find the most interesting? What about the way it works made it interesting to you? (Answers will vary.) **(make judgments)**

Writing and Research: Write a List of Facts

Activity Master, Page 24

Ask students to give examples of topics discussed in *Science Around the House.* List them on the board. Then have each student choose one topic to learn more about. If necessary, consult with students about the kinds of information they might find and where they will find it. Using their books and other sources, students will then write a list of at least four facts about their topics. Students can use the Activity Master on page 24 to help them organize their research and summarize the information they find.

Communicating: Speaking/Listening

Read a list of facts aloud

Students can read their list of facts about their topic aloud to a small group.

Students reading aloud should

✓ speak clearly and at an appropriate speed and volume

✓ make eye contact with various audience members

Listeners should

✓ listen courteously

✓ pay attention to see whether all facts directly relate to the topic

✓ ask questions to clarify main ideas

Extend and Assess

Focus on Science

Thinking Like a Scientist
Process Skill: Observing
Activity Master, Page 25

A microscope is an important tool to scientists who study extremely small objects. Using the Activity Master on page 25, students view human hair and human skin cells as they would appear under a microscope. They then answer questions about each.

Answers: 1 *Possible responses: The magnified image looks like a tube and has rough areas*
2 *Possible responses: The magnified image has a round shape, has things inside, looks soft, etc.*
3 *Answers will vary, but students might infer that scientists can learn more about structures of things and how things react to other things.*

Science and Technology: Create a Flow Chart or Diagram

Have students choose one example of technology from *Science Around the House*. They can then create a flow chart or diagram to explain how the tool or process works, including pictures as appropriate. Students should think through each step and how it relates to the next one. Then they should draw their chart or diagram, label each step, and give the chart a title. If they wish, students can include written descriptions of the process with their charts.

Assessment Options

Use the following assessment options to assess understanding of *Science Around the House*.

Questions
Ask the following questions during individual conferences or have students write the answers independently in their notebooks:

1 Identify three examples of technology in your house.

2 What happens with dust to make it bring out an allergy?

3 Explain two things that affect the way sound travels.

4 Why doesn't a remote control have to be aimed directly at a television to work?

5 What are three things in the world around you that science helps explain?

Assessment Activity
Using the contents page, have students list all of the tools or processes in *Science Around the House* in order of importance to them or their families. Students then write one sentence giving a reason for their choices of most important and least important. Suggest that students consider safety, convenience, and fun when creating their lists.

Lists should

✓ accurately list items from *Science Around the House*

✓ be ordered from most important to least important

✓ include one sentence explaining the most and least important items

Multiple-Choice Test
Use the multiple-choice test on on page 107.

Cross-Curricular Connection

Social Studies
Have students use library books, encyclopedias, or the Internet to find out about the inventors of household devices, such as vacuum cleaners, smoke detectors, remote controls, or microwaves. Have them find out who was the main inventor of one of the items and write a short biography of the person. They should include information about how the person thought the invention would improve society and people's lives.

Home-School Connection

Students can discuss the types of technology they learned about in *Science Around the House* with their families. Together, the family can locate these items in the house and discuss additional examples they find in each room. For examples, families can discuss the use of carbon monoxide detectors, conventional ovens, and cleaning supplies. Recommend that families also discuss the safety issues related to each of these examples and others found in and around the house.

Vocabulary: Determine Word Knowledge

The words below are from *Science Around the House.* Each word is related to science in your home. In the middle column, write what you already know about each word. Then use the student book and the glossary to find new information about each word. In the last column, use each word in a sentence about science you can find in your house.

Word	What I Already Know	My Sentence about Science Around the House
allergic		
filter		
microwaves		
smoke detector		
sound		
steam		

Reading: Identify Cause-and-Effect Relationships

Think about things that happen, and why they happen, in *Science Around the House*. Complete the cause-and-effect chart by listing the missing causes and effects. Remember that an effect is what happens and a cause is why it happens.

Causes	Effects
1.	1. Some people sneeze.
2.	2. Your voice sounds loud in the bathroom.
3. Microwaves hit the water in the kernel. Kernel gets very hot inside. Water turns into steam.	3.
4. Carbon dioxide is mixed in with soda. You shake up a can of soda.	4.

© 2004 National Geographic Society

Writing: Write a List of Facts

In *Science Around the House,* you read about many different ways that science works in your home. Choose one of the topics that you read about and are interested in. Find more information about this topic. Use your book, the Internet, encyclopedias, or any other source you choose. Then write a list of facts you learned about your topic. Use the questions below to guide your research.

1. What is the topic you will learn more about? _____

2. List three things you already know about this subject.

_____

_____

_____

3. What are two sources you will use to find more information?

_____

_____

4. Use the rest of the space to write information that you find as you research your topic.

_____

_____

_____

_____

_____

_____

_____

Now write your list of facts on another sheet of paper. You should have at least four facts. At the bottom of your list, write the sources you used to find the facts.

© 2004 National Geographic Society

Thinking Like a Scientist: Observing

Microscopes help scientists study very small objects such as dust mites. These objects are difficult to see using just eyes. Each of the images below is a common object. It looks the way it would appear if you observed it under a microscope. Look closely at each. Then answer the questions that follow.

Human Hair, magnified

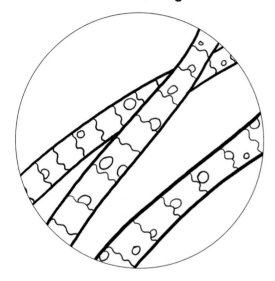

Human Skin Cells, magnified

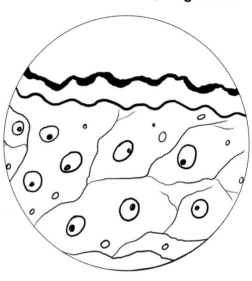

1. Look closely at the image of the magnified human hair. Now compare it to one of the hairs from your head. Write down two details in the magnified image that you cannot see on your strand of hair.

_____

_____

2. Look closely at the image of the magnified human skin cells. Write down two details from the second picture that you could not see by looking at skin on your hand.

_____

_____

3. Why might scientists want to use microscopes to see objects more closely? Think about what you've noticed here or read in the student book. Then write your answer.

_____

_____

Science Skills

Overview

Science at the Airport

By Amy Sarver

Summary

Nearly all aspects of flight and air travel involve science and the use of technology. Machines move people through the airport as well as through the air. Technology is used in airport security systems, airplane instrumentation, radar, and devices that track changes in weather. The scientific principles that shape our understanding of flight and weather help to keep airports and passengers safe.

Background Information

The historic flight of the Wright brothers' airplane in 1903 marked an important turning point in human history and technology. The Wright brothers' flight at Kitty Hawk, North Carolina, was the first successful controlled flight of a motor-driven aircraft with an on-board pilot. Since that time, airplane technology has been steadily advancing. Today, airlines are a common and convenient mode of transportation—and one that relies heavily on state-of-the-art technology. From the construction of airplanes to the security screening performed at airports, science plays an important part in the safety and flight of airplanes. Airport meteorologists across the world relay information about weather conditions to ensure the safety of air travel. Technologies using x-rays and electromagnetic metal detectors help to maximize passenger safety. The shape of an airplane wing and the fuel that powers its engines are based on fundamental scientific principles. Science and technology allow millions of people to navigate through airports and safely fly to destinations around the world.

Learning Objectives

Science

- Identify ways that science and technology are used in air transportation
- Explain how x-rays help keep airports safe
- Identify radar as a technology used in air traffic control

Process Skills

Skill Focus
- Observing

Supporting Skills
- Collecting data
- Interpreting data
- Communicating

Reading Skills

Genre: Expository
Skill Focus
- Identify main idea and details
- Use specialized words

Supporting Skills
- Summarize
- Sequence
- Identify cause-and-effect relationships

Writing Skills

Writing Focus
- Write a poem (descriptive)

Supporting Skills
- Prewrite
- Publish writing

Speaking/Listening
- Read poems aloud

Focus on Reading

Before Reading

Activate Prior Knowledge

Read the title of the book and have students look at the picture on the cover. Ask:

How might science be important at the airport?

What things might you expect to read about in a book about an airport?

Have students make a chart in their notebooks entitled *What I Expect to Learn*. Ask them to list science topics that they might learn about at an airport. Students can record facts and details about their topics as they read. They can also list facts that were new or surprising.

Preview

Give students time to look through the book paying attention to headings, subheads, and photos. When they have finished previewing the reading, ask:

What does the contents page tell you about the topics in the book?

What additional information do the subheads in each section offer?

Set Purpose

Ask students whether this book reminds them of other books they have read. Have them set a purpose for reading. Ask:

Why do you think we'll be reading this book?

Encourage students to give reasons for their answers.

Vocabulary Strategy: Use Specialized Words

Activity Master, Page 30

Explain to students that some words may be used to describe a certain topic. These words can be grouped because their meanings are related in some way. The words on the Activity Master on page 30 are specialized. All of them relate to airplanes or airports. Have students use the glossary to define each word. Then have students write one sentence to explain how each word relates to airplanes or airports. Students will use these vocabulary words:

cockpit
pictographs
radar
terminal
wind shear

What I Expect to Learn	Facts and Details
How airplanes fly	
How weather affects airplanes	
How airport security machines work	

Correlation to National Standards

Science	Reading/Language Arts	State/Local
• Properties of objects and materials (K–4) • Position and motion of objects (K–4) • Properties of Earth materials (K–4) • Changes in Earth and sky (K–4) • Science and technology (K–4) • Science in personal and social perspectives (K–4, 5–8)	• Read to build an understanding of applications of science in airports • Apply a wide range of strategies to comprehend and interpret texts • Use the writing process • Conduct research • Use written and oral language to communicate • Use a variety of informational resources	_____ _____ _____ _____ **See Standards Chart on page 101.**

During Reading

Read Strategically: Identify Main Idea and Details

Activity Master, Page 31

Assign each two-page spread of the book as independent reading. As they read, students can use the Activity Master on page 31 to list the main idea and the details that support it in several sections.

Remind students that the main idea is the most important idea, and the details are facts or other pieces of information that tell more about the main idea. Students might turn each main idea into a question and then read to find details to answer it. The details they choose should tell more about the main idea.

Strategy Tip: Take notes

Students may want to take notes to help them understand all the information in the text. You could have them set up an outline or other form based on the page headings. Alternatively, students could make bookmarks out of notebook paper and take notes on the bookmarks as they read. Encourage them to use their notes to review the main concepts of the book.

Meeting Individual Needs

For specific strategies on meeting individual needs, see pages 90–95.

After Reading

Responding

Initiate a class discussion to assess reading comprehension. Ask:

Why are pictographs used to communicate with airport travelers instead of signs with words? Note: Pictographs on page 7 of student book depict (from left to right) a water fountain, telephone, elevator, and airport security. (See pages 6–7 in the student book.) **(summarize)**

Describe the steps involved in tracking your luggage at an airport. (See pages 8–9.) **(sequence)**

What might happen if a coin is passed through an airport metal detector? (See pages 10–11.) **(identify cause-and-effect relationships)**

What are some ways that help people move quickly from one part of an airport to another? (See pages 12–13.) **(summarize)**

In general, what kinds of weather conditions might make airplane flights dangerous? (See pages 14–15.) **(make generalizations)**

Writing and Research: Write a Poem

Activity Master, Page 32

Ask students to close their eyes and imagine themselves in the terminal of an airport. It could be an airport they have visited or one they have learned about through research. You might begin by having students look through the pictures in this book or by showing other pictures of airports to students to prompt their thinking. Ask students to picture in their minds what they can see, hear, smell, taste, and touch at an airport. Then have students use the Activity Master on page 32 to record their thoughts. Students can use these ideas to write a poem. Remind them that a poem should create an overall feeling or impression.

Communicating: Speaking/Listening

Read poems aloud

After writing their poems, students may want to work with partners to revise them. Partners should offer suggestions on how to write clearer images that evoke strong feelings. After revisions have been made, invite students to practice reading their poems aloud and then have them present the poems for a small group.

Students reading aloud should

✓ speak clearly

✓ emphasize important words

✓ make eye contact with the audience

Listeners should

✓ show polite attention by making eye contact and listening quietly

✓ identify images that were particularly strong or well written

✓ explain what the poem made them feel

Extend and Assess

Focus on Science

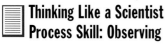

Thinking Like a Scientist
Process Skill: Observing
Activity Master, Page 33

Scientists often observe objects, organisms, and events through careful examination. Ask students to imagine that they are scientists who are observing what happens at an airport. Students can record their findings on the Activity Master on page 33.

Answers: *Student responses will vary.*

Physical Science: Create a Venn Diagram

Have students review information in the book about x-rays and radar. They can create a Venn diagram like the one below to compare and contrast x-rays and radar and how they are used to keep people safe at the airport. Remind students to write details specific to x-rays or radar in the part of the circles that do not overlap and write details that apply to both in the overlapping areas.

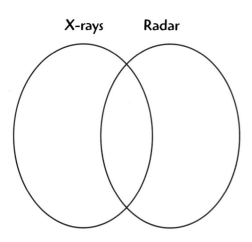

Assessment Options

Use the following assessment options to assess students' understanding of *Science at the Airport.*

Questions

Use the following questions during individual conferences or ask students to write answers in their notebooks.

1 Identify four ways science and technology are used at airports.

2 Explain how airports use x-rays to help keep people safe.

3 How does radar help control traffic at airports?

4 How does lift allow airplanes to fly?

5 What jobs do people do at the airport? What does each person do?

Assessment Activity

Have students write a book review of *Science at the Airport.* Remind them to support opinions with information from the book. Students should answer these questions to complete their reviews:

What is your favorite part of the book? Why?

Explain three things that you learned from the book.

Was there anything you expected the book to discuss that it didn't? If so, what?

Would you recommend this book to a friend? Why or why not?

Book reviews should

✓ address each question

✓ include accurate information

✓ support opinions with details from the text, when applicable

✓ give reasons to support their opinions

Multiple-Choice Test

Use the multiple-choice test on page 108.

Cross-Curricular Connection

Art

Have students identify signs from the book—water fountain, telephone, elevator, and security—that might be appropriate for use in their school. Next ask students to identify places in their school—restrooms, cafeteria, gymnasium, principal or nurse's office—where similar pictographs might be useful. Ask students to create pictographs for the areas they identify. Then have them share their drawings with the class, asking other students to guess the meanings of the signs.

Home-School Connection

Have students discuss the types of pictographs they learned about in *Science at the Airport* with their families. Together, the family can discuss other places in the community (or even plan trips to them) that make use of pictographs. Have students draw and identify the meanings of the pictographs they see around their community and identify where each was used. Students can use their drawings to make a pictograph scrapbook.

Vocabulary: Use Specialized Words

The words below are from *Science at the Airport*. First, use your glossary to define each word. Then write a sentence explaining what each word has to do with airplanes or airports.

1. cockpit

Definition: _____

My sentence: _____

_____

2. pictographs

Definition: _____

My sentence: _____

_____

3. radar

Definition: _____

My sentence: _____

_____

4. terminal

Definition: _____

My sentence: _____

_____

5. wind shear

Definition: _____

My sentence: _____

_____

Reading: Identify Main Idea and Details

The main idea is what a paragraph or chapter is mostly about. Details are pieces of information that tell more about a main idea. Complete the chart below, adding main ideas and details.

Pages 6–7

Main Idea: To communicate with travelers, airport planners use pictographs.

Details:

•

•

Pages 8–9

Main Idea:

Details:

•

•

Pages 10–11

Main Idea: At the airport, security is serious business.

Details:

•

•

Pages 14–15

Main Idea: Keeping track of the weather is a top priority at the airport.

Details:

•

•

Pages 16–17

Main Idea:

Details:

•

•

Pages 18–19

Main Idea: Pilots get their directions from air traffic controllers.

Details:

•

•

Writing: Write a Poem

Imagine a trip to the airport—an airport that you have visited or heard about. What is it like in an airport? Use your book, the Internet, or other resources, such as videotapes or movies, to get ideas. What might you see, hear, smell, taste, and feel? Write a poem about being at an airport and use words that help others imagine what the airport is like.

Remember that poems do not have to rhyme, but they should use words that help others imagine what you are describing. Use the space below to organize your ideas for writing. Remember to give your poem a title.

1. Write four things your might see at an airport:

    _____   _____

    _____   _____

2. Write four things you might hear at an airport:

    _____   _____

    _____   _____

3. Write two things you might smell at an airport:

    _____   _____

4. Write two things you might taste at an airport:

    _____   _____

5. Write two activities you might do at an airport:

    _____   _____

    The title of my poem is _____

On a separate sheet of paper, choose one thing from each group above. Write a sentence about your choice. You can put your sentences together to begin your poem. Choose words that help each sentence describe the airport!

Thinking Like a Scientist: Observing

Think of an airport you have been to or researched. In the first box, write what you observed. In the second box, draw a picture of at least one of the words you have written in the first box. In the third box, write one fact you learned about an item you drew.

My list of what I saw at the airport:

My sketches of what I saw at the airport:

My fact:

© 2004 National Geographic Society

Overview

Science at the Aquarium

By Kate Boehm Jerome

Summary

Aquariums are human-made water environments. These environments provide the creatures that live there with everything they need to survive. Aquariums help protect wildlife for future generations. Aquariums display plants and vertebrate and invertebrate animals. These organisms have specific needs that require them to be grouped with compatible organisms and kept in displays that are maintained at certain temperatures. People work together to maintain aquariums and care for the animals that live there. This work results in displays that allow people to learn more about water creatures and their environments and also helps protect injured animals and species that are in danger of dying out.

Science Background

Aquariums are very popular public institutions. According to the American Zoo and Aquarium Association (AZA), more people visit zoos and aquariums in the United States than attend all the NFL, NBA, and major league baseball games combined. Modern aquariums participate in many important conservation programs, including species survival plans, aquatic research and rescue projects, and marine education programs for the general public. Most aquariums rely on volunteers to supplement their caretaking staff. Volunteers perform duties ranging from food preparation to leading group tours. Most aquariums have special programs for teachers and students.

Learning Objectives

Science

- Recognize that many plants and animals live in water habitats
- Understand that animals with different needs have different habitats
- Identify structures that are unique to different ocean animals
- Define adaptation

Process Skills

Skill Focus
- Creating a graph

Supporting Skills
- Interpreting data
- Communicating

Reading Skills

Genre: Expository
Skill Focus
- Identify main idea and details
- Use context clues

Supporting Skills
- Paraphrase
- Compare and contrast
- Summarize

Writing Skills

Writing Focus
- Write an adventure story (narrative)

Supporting Skills
- Prewrite
- Use the writing process

Speaking and Listening
- Give an oral presentation

Focus on Reading

Before Reading

Activate Prior Knowledge

Direct students' attention to the cover of the student book and the book title. Ask:

What is the young person in the cover photograph doing?

What is an aquarium?

Ask volunteers to describe any experiences they have had while visiting an aquarium. Then tell students that this book is about aquariums and why they are important. It examines the types of living things that are kept in aquariums, the work of the people who care for the living things, and how aquariums can help people conserve or protect wildlife from extinction.

Preview

Give students time to flip through the book. Tell them to pay particular attention to section titles, photographs, and special features. Ask:

From reading the section titles, can you predict what this book is about?

Look at the photographs used in the book. What kind of information do the photographs provide?

Set Purpose

Ask students whether this book reminds them of other books they have read. Have them set a purpose for reading. Ask:

Why do you think you'll be reading this book?

Encourage students to give reasons for their answers. Have them set a purpose for reading, such as *I want to read to find out what kinds of things live in water environments.*

Vocabulary Strategy: Use Context Clues

Activity Master, Page 38

Have students turn to page 8 in their books. Point out the word *tentacles* and have a volunteer read the paragraph containing that word. Ask:

Can you figure out what the word tentacles *means by reading the sentence that contains the word?*

Explain that using context clues, the words or sentences around an unknown word, is a good strategy for finding the meaning of words. Have students use *Science at the Aquarium* to complete the Activity Master on page 38. Students write a definition for each word based on context clues and then use the glossary to check their answers. Students will use these words:

habitat
invertebrate
mammal

Correlation to National Standards

Science	Reading/Language Arts	State/Local
• Characteristics of organisms (K–4) • Organisms and environments (K–4) • Scientific inquiry (K–4) • Science as a human endeavor (K–4) • Science and technology (K–4)	• Read to be informed • Apply a range of strategies to comprehend and interpret text • Apply language structures and conventions • Use the writing process • Conduct research • Use a variety of informational resources	_____ _____ _____ _____

See Standards Chart on page 101.

During Reading

 ### Read Strategically: Identify Main Idea and Details

Activity Master, Page 39

Assign each chapter of the book as independent reading. Have students use the Activity Master on page 39 as a study guide to help them identify main ideas of various sections. On the Activity Master, students provide supporting details for the main ideas of the sections they are given. For the remaining sections, students write both the main idea and the supporting details. Remind students that in order to find the main idea, they should ask themselves what the section is mostly about. They might then turn each main idea statement into a question and read to find details to answer the question.

Strategy Tip: Paraphrase

If students have difficulty understanding a sentence or a group of sentences in the book, suggest that they paraphrase, or retell in their own words, that part of the book. Explain that paraphrasing helps identify what parts of the text they don't understand. If students continue to have difficulty understanding certain passages, they can ask for help during class discussion.

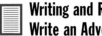 ### Meeting Individual Needs

For specific strategies on meeting individual needs, see pages 90–95.

After Reading

Responding

Initiate a class discussion to assess reading comprehension. Ask:

What is a habitat? (See page 4 in the student book.) **(identify main idea and details)**

Why are some animals kept in separate exhibits at an aquarium? (See pages 6–7.) **(summarize)**

How do jellyfish differ from fish? (See page 8.) **(compare and contrast)**

How is the way a jellyfish breathes different from the way a whale breathes? (See pages 8 and 10.) **(compare and contrast)**

What kind of jobs must people at an aquarium do? (See pages 12–13.) **(summarize)**

Why do some fish swim in groups called schools? (See pages 14–15.) **(summarize)**

What adaptations does an octopus have that a shark does not? (See page 16.) **(compare and contrast)**

What may happen if small baby fish are not removed from a tank containing large fish? (See page 18.) **(identify cause-and-effect relationships)**

What are some ways aquariums help conserve plants and animals? (See page 20.) **(summarize)**

Writing and Research: Write an Adventure Story

Activity Master, Page 40

Tell students that they are going to write an adventure story that takes place in an aquarium. The stories should include some facts they learned about aquariums and the animals who live there. The Activity Master on page 40 will help students organize their ideas.

Communicating: Speaking/Listening

Give an oral presentation

Have students read their stories aloud.

Students reading aloud should

✓ speak clearly

✓ make eye contact with listeners

✓ adapt speech as appropriate

Listeners should

✓ listen politely

✓ ask questions to clarify the plot

✓ listen for facts related to aquariums

Extend and Assess

Focus on Science

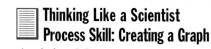 **Thinking Like a Scientist**
Process Skill: Creating a Graph
Activity Master, Page 41

The approximate lengths of eight types of whales, including the beluga whale students read about in *Science at the Aquarium*, are listed in a chart on the Activity Master on page 41. Students use this information to create and label a bar graph. Students then use the graph to answer questions.

Answers: 1 *beluga* **2** *fin*
3 *65 feet*

Life Science: Create an Adaptations Poster

Remind students that an adaptation is a structure or behavior that helps an animal survive in its environment. The adaptations of several animals are discussed or shown in *Science at the Aquarium*. Have students prepare a poster that shows at least three adaptations of animals from *Science at the Aquarium*. They can draw pictures or find them in magazines and compare. Students should add labels or captions to identify the adaptations shown and tell in a few words how the adaptation helps the animal survive. Have students title their posters.

Assessment Options

Use the following assessment options to assess students' understanding of *Science at the Aquarium*.

Questions

Use the following questions during individual conferences, or ask students to write answers in their notebooks.

1 Why don't aquarists put all the animals on display at an aquarium in the same tank?

2 What is one main difference between jellyfish and fish?

3 How does the job of an aquarist differ from that of a veterinarian?

4 What are two reasons fish swim in schools?

5 What are some ways aquariums help conserve ocean animals?

Assessment Activity

Have students use magazines and newspapers or create drawings to represent one of the following concepts from *Science at the Aquarium*.

- Different animals and plants have different needs.

- Fish swim in schools, or groups, for several reasons.

- Special characteristics, called adaptations, help all animals survive in their habitats.

Pictures should

✓ clearly address concept

✓ use words and images to communicate ideas

✓ be well-organized and carefully prepared

Multiple-Choice Test

Use the multiple-choice test on page 109.

Cross-Curricular Connection

Social Studies

Oceans are large saltwater environments. Students can use reference books and the Internet to find the names of the world's oceans. Then students can trace a map of the world. Students should clearly label the oceans on their map.

Home-School Connection

Students can share with their families information they learned in *Science at the Aquarium*. They can discuss with parents their favorite topic and observations about information they read in the book.

Vocabulary: Use Context Clues

The words below are from *Science at the Aquarium*. Find each word in the book and read the paragraph that contains the word. In the second column in the chart below, write a definition for each word based on how it is used in the paragraph. In the third column, write the definition from the glossary.

Word	Definition from Context Clues	Definition from Glossary
habitat		
invertebrate		
mammal		

Reading: Identify Main Idea and Details

The main idea of a section is what that section is mostly about. Details are facts and examples that explain or support the main idea. Complete the chart by filling in details and main ideas for the sections listed. Your chart should contain one main idea and three supporting details.

Habitats, pp. 6–7 **Main Idea:** Some animals in an aquarium are kept separate from others.

Details
-
-
-

Marine Mammals, pp. 10–11 **Main Idea:** Whales come to the surface to get air.

Details
-
-
-

Aquarium Caretakers, p. 12–13 **Main Idea:**

Details
-
-
-

Adaptations, p. 16 **Main Idea:**

Details
-
-
-

© 2004 National Geographic Society

Writing: Write an Adventure Story

You will be writing an adventure story that takes place in an aquarium. Your story should have characters, a plot, and describe the aquarium and its contents. Plan your story below.

1. Describe the aquarium where your story takes place. _____

_____

_____

2. What characters will be in your story? _____

_____

3. Identify a problem the characters will have. Explain how they will they solve the problem.

_____

_____

_____

4. What kinds of equipment (tools or technology) will your characters use to move about the aquarium or solve their problem?

_____

_____

_____

5. What kinds of plants and animals live in the aquarium? What do these plants and animals look like and how will they be important to the story?

_____

_____

_____

6. How will your story end? _____

_____

Writing

© 2004 National Geographic Society

Thinking Like a Scientist: Creating a Graph

One type of animal you may see at an aquarium is a whale. Whales, like the beluga whales you read about in *Science at the Aquarium,* are among the largest ocean animals. However, whales come in many different sizes. The chart below tells the approximate lengths of eight types of whales. Use this information to label each bar in the graph with the name of the whale it describes. The first two are done for you. Then write a title for your graph on the line provided.

Whale	Length
Beluga	17 feet
Humpback	49 feet
Gray	39 feet
Minke	29 feet
Orca	32 feet
Right	56 feet
Fin	82 feet
Pilot	27 feet

Title: _____

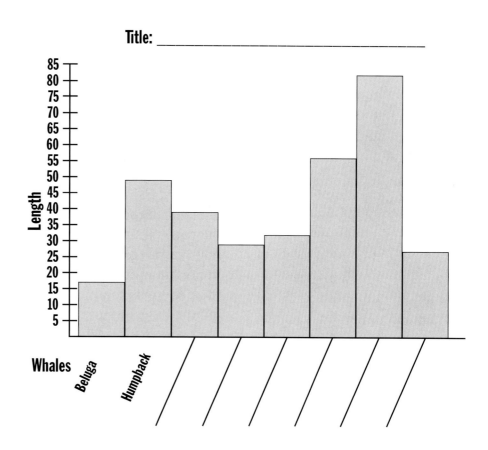

Use your graph to answer the following questions.

1. Which whale on your graph is the shortest? _____

2. Which whale is the longest? _____

3. What is the difference in length between the shortest and the longest whale on your graph?

_____

Overview

Science at the Grocery

By Amy Sarver

Summary

In order to keep foods fresh and well preserved, grocery stores depend on science and technology. Pasteurization helps kill bacteria in milk and allows milk to last longer without spoiling. Irrigation systems spray vegetables with water to keep them fresh. Technology is used in freezers, refrigerators, and even the automatic doors of the grocery store. Scanners, lasers, and computers work together to help make checkout faster for the customer and the cashier. On their scientific tour of the grocery, students learn how classification is important at the grocery store and why foods are grouped together in certain ways. The nutritional information on food labels is explored. Students also learn the advantages and disadvantages of choosing paper or plastic.

Science Background

As students will learn by reading *Science at the Grocery*, even a trip to the grocery store is filled with science and technology. The classification of foods in the grocery store and the nutritional information on food labels are examples of life science in action. Other examples of science at the grocery involve technology. For example, light bouncing off objects can tell a sensor to open a door. Temperature can be raised or lowered to kill germs and preserve food. People have also found ways to use technology to make the check out process faster and more accurate. These examples help students recognize that science extends to all parts of their daily lives.

Learning Objectives

Science

- Identify examples of science and technology in a setting familiar to many students
- Identify technologies that keep food fresh
- Explain the use of lasers and bar codes in grocery stores

Process Skills

Skill Focus
- Classifying

Supporting Skills
- Collecting data
- Communicating
- Inferring

Reading Skills

Genre: Expository
Skill Focus
- Make generalizations
- Use context clues

Supporting Skills
- Classify
- Compare and contrast
- Summarize
- Draw conclusions

Writing Skills

Writing Focus
- Write a list of facts (expository)

Supporting Skills
- Conduct research
- Prewrite

Speaking/Listening
- Give an oral presentation

Focus on Reading

Before Reading

Activate Prior Knowledge

Read the title of the book and have students look at the picture on the cover. Ask:

What scientific things do you think you might find in a grocery store?

What kinds of technology (machines or devices) might you see in a grocery store?

Have students make a chart in their notebooks titled *What I Expect to Learn*. Ask them to write things they think they will learn about science and technology in a grocery. Students can record facts and details about their topics as they read. They can also list facts that are new and surprising.

Preview

Give students time to flip through the book, paying attention to headings, subheadings, and photos. When they have finished previewing the reading, ask:

What might you learn from the photographs?

What can you learn from the subheadings used in this book?

Set Purpose

Ask students how this book reminds them of other books they have read. Have them set a purpose for reading. Ask:

What do you want to find out as you read?

Encourage students to give reasons for their answers.

Vocabulary Strategy: Use Context Clues
Activity Master, Page 46

Have students turn to page 19 in the student book. Point out the word *laser* and have a volunteer read the sentence that contains that word. Ask students to use words and sentences before and after the word to figure out the meaning of *laser:*

Explain that using context clues—the words and sentences that come before and after an unknown word—is a good strategy for understanding a word's meaning. Students can use context clues with the Activity Master on page 46 to define vocabulary words. They can then compare their definitions to the glossary definitions. Students will use these words:

laser
physical change
recycled
sensor

What I Expect to Learn	Facts and Details
How food is kept fresh	
What important things are in food	

Correlation to National Standards

Science	Reading/Language Arts	State/Local
• Properties of objects and materials (K–4) • Light, heat, electricity, and magnetism (K–4) • Science and technology (K–4) • Personal health (K–4) • Science and technology in local challenges (K–4)	• Read to build an understanding of how science is used in the grocery • Apply a wide range of strategies to comprehend and interpret texts • Conduct research • Use the writing process • Use written and oral language to communicate • Use a variety of informational resources	_____ _____ _____ _____ **See Standards Chart on page 101.**

During Reading

 Read Strategically: Make Generalizations

Activity Master, Page 47

Assign each two-page spread of the book as independent reading. As students read, they should make generalizations about information presented in the text. Students can then use the Activity Master on page 47 to write examples supporting the generalizations provided.

Remind students that a generalization is a rule that applies to many examples. Encourage students to look for words like *most, many, some, generally,* and *few.*

Strategy Tip: Reread

Each section of *Science at the Grocery* is organized around an opening question that introduces a main topic. If students need help understanding these topics, encourage them to reread information that addresses the opening question.

Meeting Individual Needs

For specific strategies on meeting individual needs, see pages 90–95.

After Reading

Responding

Initiate a class discussion to assess reading comprehension. Ask:

What makes the doors at the grocery store move all by themselves? (See page 6 in the student book.) **(identify cause-and-effect relationships)**

Where would you look for fresh carrots in a grocery store? (See pages 8–9.) **(draw conclusions)**

What are some ways different foods are kept fresh? (See pages 10–12.) **(compare and contrast)**

What kind of information is found on a food label? (See pages 16–17.) **(summarize)**

How do lasers and computers work together to interpret bar codes? (See pages 18–19.) **(summarize)**

How does technology help a busy shopper have more time for other things? (Answers will vary.) **(draw conclusions)**

Writing and Research: Write a List of Facts

Activity Master, Page 48

Ask students to give examples of topics discussed in *Science at the Grocery.* List the topics on the board. Then have each student select one topic to research. If necessary, consult with students about the kinds of information they might find and where they will conduct their research. Using their books and other sources, students will then write a list of at least four facts about their topic. Students can use the Activity Master on page 48 to help them organize their research and summarize the information they find.

Communicating: Speaking/Listening

Give an oral presentation

Have students work in small groups and take turns reading aloud the information about their topics.

Students reading aloud should

✓ speak clearly and at an appropriate speed and volume

✓ make eye contact with listeners

Listeners should

✓ listen politely

✓ pay attention to see whether all facts directly relate to the topic

✓ ask questions to clarify facts

Extend and Assess

Focus on Science

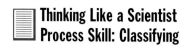 **Thinking Like a Scientist**
Process Skill: Classifying
Activity Master, Page 49

Items in a grocery are usually classified, or grouped together, based on their similarities. Groceries use signs above aisles to help shoppers find what they need. Sample grocery signs are shown on the Activity Master on page 49. Students are asked to use the signs to help identify where in the store each item on a shopping list might be found. Then have students rewrite the list to show what items they would group together and explain why.

Life Science: Simple Chart

Drawing on their own experiences, students can create simple charts that list types of items they would expect to find in grocery store aisles and specific foods that would be found in each aisle. Have each student draw a chart in his or her notebook and complete it. Remind students to list items that are different from those on the Activity Master.

Assessment Options

Use the following assessment options to assess students' understanding of *Science at the Grocery.*

Questions

Use the following questions during individual conferencing or ask students to write answers in their notebooks.

1 What are some examples of technology that are used in a grocery store?

2 What are some things in a grocery store that come from nature?

3 How are items arranged in a grocery store? Why is the arrangement important?

4 What types of tools are used to record information about products in a grocery store?

5 How is science used to help keep food fresh?

Assessment Activity

Have students choose a label from a food product. Students can use this label as a sample and make a poster that illustrates and explains the information that is often included on food labels. Posters should include captions and labels that identify the type of information shown on the label and explain why the information is important.

Posters should

✓ accurately explain what information is presented in a food label

✓ be carefully prepared

Captions should

✓ address all required topics

✓ present information clearly

✓ be accurate

✓ use correct grammar and mechanics

Multiple-Choice Test

Use the multiple-choice test on page 110.

Cross-Curricular Connection

Social Studies

Foods sold in grocery stores come from many different locations. Have students conduct research to find out what food products are frequently grown or raised in five different states. Students can draw maps of the states they research. On each map, they should record the name of the state and list three food products produced by that state. Students can combine their completed pages with those of other students to make a class booklet titled *Food Products of the United States.*

Home-School Connection

With their families, students can discuss what they learned while reading *Science at the Grocery.* Together, the family can discuss how groceries are stored once they are brought home and why some items are stored in different places.

Vocabulary: Use Context Clues

Read the sentences below. The underlined words are from *Science at the Grocery*. Use the context clues, or words around each underlined word, to help you write a definition for the underlined word. Then look up the word in the glossary and write the glossary definition.

1. A scanner uses <u>laser</u> light to read the bar codes. The laser light moves across the dark and light areas of the bar code.

Meaning from context: _____

_____

Meaning from glossary: _____

_____

2. When ice melts, a <u>physical change</u> happens. It may change shape and turn into a liquid, but it is still the same substance—ice cream.

Meaning from context: _____

_____

Meaning from glossary: _____

_____

3. Paper bags can be <u>recycled</u> and made into new paper products.

Meaning from context: _____

_____

Meaning from glossary: _____

_____

4. Some automatic doors use a <u>sensor</u> to tell when something is near.

Meaning from context: _____

_____

Meaning from glossary: _____

_____

Reading: Make Generalizations

A generalization is a general conclusion, or statement. Often, generalizations use words like *most, many, some, generally,* and *few.* Read each generalization about the topics in *Science at the Grocery.* Find examples in the book that support each generalization.

Generalization: Many foods are frozen so that they last longer.

Examples:

-
-
-

Generalization: A grocery store uses many kinds of technology to make shopping quicker and easier.

Examples:

-
-
-

Generalization: In a grocery store, similar items are often grouped together.

Examples:

-
-
-

Generalization: Many communities have recycling programs.

Examples:

-
-
-

Name _____

Writing: Write a List of Facts

In *Science at the Grocery,* you read about many scientific topics. Choose one topic that interests you and find more information about this topic. You can use your book, the Internet, encyclopedias, or any other source you choose. Then write a list of facts you have learned about your topic. Use the questions below to guide your research.

1. What is the topic you will learn more about? _____

2. List three things you already know about this subject.

_____

_____

_____

3. What are two sources you will use to find more information?

_____

_____

4. On the lines provided, list facts you learned about your topic. At the bottom of your list, write the sources you used to find these facts.

_____

_____

_____

_____

_____

_____

_____

_____

Thinking Like a Scientist: Classifying

The signs below tell what items are in five grocery store aisles. Use the signs to decide where each item on the shopping list will most likely be located. Write the aisle number in the space provided beside each item. Remember that grocery stores usually classify, or group, similar items together. This makes shopping easier.

Shopping List

oatmeal _____

spaghetti _____

cheese _____

hot dogs _____

apples _____

sugar _____

ice cream _____

lettuce _____

breakfast bars _____

cake mix _____

carrots _____

popsicles _____

tomato sauce _____

chicken noodle soup _____

Aisle 1	Aisle 2	Aisle 3	Aisle 4	Aisle 5
Fruits and Vegetables	Cereals, Spices, and Baking Items	Canned Foods, Soups, Sauces, and Pastas	Frozen Foods Packaged Meats	Dairy, Eggs

1. On the lines provided, rewrite your list, placing items in the same aisles together.

_____

_____

_____

_____

2. Now create a new shopping list with foods different from those on the list above. Classify the new items based on the aisles where they would be found.

_____

_____

_____

© 2004 National Geographic Society

Science Skills

Overview

Science at the Mall

By Amy Sarver

Summary

Although malls are usually thought of as commercial centers, they are also sites for exploring science. Many state-of-the-art technologies are used to make malls safe and efficient for shoppers and store owners. Within the mall, students can identify escalators as an example of the use of motors to move large numbers of people. Neon lights and store mirrors serve as topics for discussing the properties of light. Headphones in music stores allow students to discover how sound travels. Everything from store security systems to motion-activated faucets encourages students to take a closer look at the science and technology that shape their lives. As students consider these amenities to modern living, they are also reminded of the importance of conservation and are introduced to ways that people can reduce their use of energy.

Science Background

A shopping mall doesn't immediately bring science to mind. For this reason, the mall serves as a perfect site for exploring the role of science in our everyday lives. Nearly everything in the mall—from mirrors to the security tags used in stores—relies upon science. By exploring the mall, students will gain knowledge of many basic principles in physical science. They will learn how light travels by examining their reflections in store mirrors. Music stores become science centers for exploring sound. Neon lights illustrate the properties of some gases, while investigating making chocolate offers an opportunity to discuss liquids and solids. Science and technology are integral to many facets of the structure and function of shopping malls.

Learning Objectives

Science	Process Skills	Reading Skills	Writing Skills
• Tell how light helps you see yourself in a mirror • Explain what causes sound • Describe how radio signals are used in mall security systems • Identify ways to conserve energy	**Skill Focus** • Observing **Supporting Skills** • Communicating • Collecting data • Inferring	**Genre: Expository** **Skill Focus** • Draw conclusions • Relate words **Supporting Skills** • Summarize • Use images to aid comprehension	**Writing Focus** • Write steps in a process (expository) **Supporting Skills** • Prewrite • Conduct research **Viewing** • Illustrate steps in a process

Focus on Reading

Before Reading

Activate Prior Knowledge

Ask students to think about the different forms of energy and ways they use each form in their daily lives. You might ask questions such as these:

What are some forms of energy?

What are some ways you use each form of energy?

Create a web on the board to organize students' ideas. Have students complete a similar web in their notebooks. Encourage students to add to their webs as they read *Science at the Mall*. At the conclusion of the book, have students share their ideas with the class.

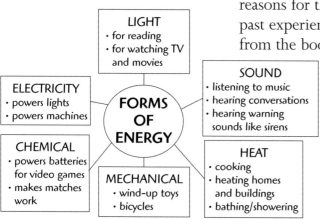

Preview

Give students time to flip through the book, paying attention to section titles, headings, and photographs. Ask:

From reading the section titles, can you predict what this book will be about?

What is shown in the photographs used in the book?

Set Purpose

Ask students whether this book reminds them of other books they have read. Have them set a purpose for reading. Ask:

What do you want to find out as you read?

Encourage students to give reasons for their answers, using past experiences or images from the book as examples.

Vocabulary Strategy: Relate Words

Activity Master, Page 54

Have students turn to pages 4 and 5 in the student book. Read the two pages to the class. Point out the word *technology* and explain to students that technology is the practical use of science in everyday life. Then ask:

Where can you find examples of science and technology at the mall?

Explain to students that the vocabulary words on the Activity Master on page 54 relate to science and technology in shopping malls. Have students use the glossary to give the meaning of each word and then write a sentence relating the word to how it is used at the mall. Students will be using these words:

infrared light
machine
mirror
neon light
sound

Correlation to National Standards

Science	Reading/Language Arts	State/Local
• Properties of objects and materials (K–4) • Light, heat, electricity, and magnetism (K–4) • Science and technology (K–4) • Science as a human endeavor (K–4) • Scientific inquiry (K–4)	• Read to be informed • Apply a range of strategies to comprehend and interpret texts • Connect ideas across texts • Use the writing process	_____ _____ _____ _____

See Standards Chart on page 101.

During Reading

📖 Read Strategically: Draw Conclusions

Activity Master, Page 55

Assign each chapter of the book as independent reading. As they read, students can use the Activity Master on page 55 to draw conclusions about ways that science is used at the mall. Explain that students draw conclusions every day. Remind them that when they draw conclusions, they make a decision about something, using the facts they're given and what they already know. In this case, they'll draw conclusions based on the facts in the book.

Strategy Tip: Use images to aid comprehension

Every image in *Science at the Mall* supports the text in some way. Suggest that students "read" the photos as they read the text to help them more fully comprehend the book. They can ask questions as they do this:

How do the large photos go with the text?

What part of the text do the smaller photos help explain?

👤 Meeting Individual Needs

For specific strategies on meeting individual needs, see pages 90–95.

After Reading

Responding

Initiate a class discussion to assess reading comprehension. Ask:

What is a machine? What machines are discussed in this book? (See pages 6 and 18 in the student book.) **(summarize)**

How are neon lights different from other lights? (See page 8.) **(compare and contrast)**

How does reflected light allow you to see things? (See page 10.) **(draw conclusions)**

What causes sound? (See page 12.) **(summarize)**

What causes the alarm on a security tag to go off? (See pages 14–15.) **(identify cause-and-effect relationships)**

Why is temperature important in the making of chocolate? (See page 17.) **(summarize)**

Why does an infrared faucet turn off when you move your hands out from under the faucet? (See page 18.) **(identify cause-and-effect relationships)**

What are some ways that people conserve energy at the mall? (See page 20.) **(summarize)**

📖 Writing and Research: Steps in a Process

Activity Master, Page 56

Discuss with students how the making of a chocolate bar involves many steps—from the picking of the cocoa beans to the cooling and hardening of chocolate in a mold. Students can list the steps involved in the making of a chocolate bar, using the student book and other resources to help clarify their understanding of this process. Have students use the Activity Master on page 56 to help them organize their ideas.

Communicating: Viewing

Illustrate steps in a process

Students can create illustrated panels to accompany each step in the chocolate-making process described in their writing.

Students should use color, labels, and captions to enhance the meaning of their illustrations.

Illustrations should

✓ explain and enhance the meaning in each written step of the chocolate-making process

✓ include captions, labels, and color

✓ use correct grammar and mechanics

Extend and Assess

Focus on Science

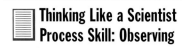 **Thinking Like a Scientist**
Process Skill: Observing
Activity Master, Page 57

During scientific investigations, scientists make observations. This means they carefully use their senses to gather information about the objects, organisms, or events they are studying. Ask students to imagine that they are scientists who are making observations at a busy shopping mall. Have them record observations they would expect to make at a mall on the Activity Master, page 57.

Answers: *Students observations will vary.*

Science and Technology: Create a Diagram

Have students choose one example of technology from *Science at the Mall.* Each student should then create a diagram that explains how the technology works. Encourage students to include a picture of the technology and ordered steps or pictures that explain how the technology operates. Students can use *Science at the Mall,* the Internet, or other resources to learn more about the chosen topic. Students should include labels or written descriptions of the technology shown on their diagrams.

Assessment Options

Use the following assessment options to assess students' understanding of *Science at the Mall.*

Questions

Use the following questions during individual conferences or ask students to write answers in their notebooks.

1 Why is an escalator an example of a machine?

2 How do neon lights differ from the lights you use in your home?

3 How do mirrors allow you to see an image of yourself?

4 How does infrared light differ from the light used in a neon display?

5 What does it mean to conserve energy?

Assessment Activity

Have students create an illustrated dictionary of seven important terms from *Science at the Mall.* Students can use pictures from magazines or they can draw pictures.

Dictionaries should

✓ include at least seven entries with matching text and images

✓ use alphabetical order

✓ be accurate and carefully prepared

✓ use correct grammar and mechanics

Multiple-Choice Test

Use the multiple-choice test on page 111.

Cross-Curricular Connection

Social Studies

Ask students to think about and identify other places in their community that make use of the same types of devices or technology as those discussed in *Science at the Mall.* Students can present their findings in a graphic manner, such as in a chart, an illustration, or a map of their community.

Home-School Connection

Students can find newspaper advertisements featuring items that use electricity, light, or sound. Have students work with family members to write a sentence about two or more products that explains how electricity, light, or sound is important to the products.

Vocabulary: Relate Words

The words below are from *Science at the Mall*. Each word has something to do with technology, or the practical use of science. Write the meaning of each word and use the glossary to check your understanding. Then write a sentence for each word that shows you how the word relates to a way that science is used at the mall.

Word	Meaning	My Sentence
infrared light		
machine		
mirror		
neon light		
sound		

Reading: Draw Conclusions

When you draw a conclusion, you make a decision about something based on the information you are given and on what you already know. Write answers to these questions to draw conclusions.

1. Besides escalators, what other machines help people travel from place to place?

    _____

    _____

2. What are some ways electricity is used at the mall?

    _____

    _____

3. Given what you know about mirrors, why are dressing rooms at the mall well lit?

    _____

    _____

4. What must happen in an object for it to produce sound?

    _____

    _____

5. What does an antenna do?

    _____

    _____

6. How is energy used in the making of chocolate?

    _____

    _____

7. Why is it important to conserve energy?

    _____

    _____

© 2004 National Geographic Society

Writing: Steps in a Process

The process of making of a chocolate bar involves many steps, from the picking of the cocoa beans to the hardening of the chocolate in a mold. Writing a description of these steps can help you understand the chocolate-making process. You can use *Science at the Mall,* the Internet, and other resources to make sure you understand the steps in this process. When writing each step, focus on the most important idea. Use the spaces below to organize the steps in a process.

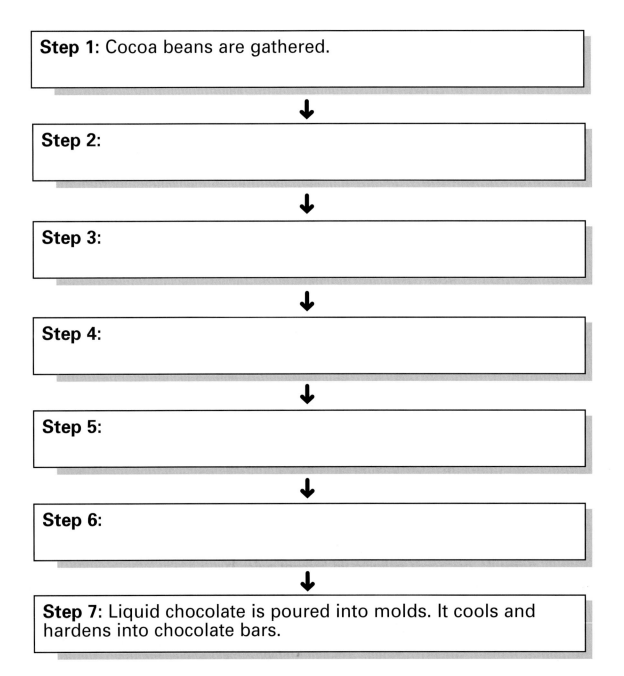

Step 1: Cocoa beans are gathered.

↓

Step 2:

↓

Step 3:

↓

Step 4:

↓

Step 5:

↓

Step 6:

↓

Step 7: Liquid chocolate is poured into molds. It cools and hardens into chocolate bars.

Thinking Like a Scientist: Observing

You use your senses—sight, smell, taste, hearing, and touch—to learn about your surroundings. Using your senses to gather information is called observing. Imagine that you are a scientist making observations in a busy shopping mall. Think about things at a mall that you can see, smell, taste, hear, and touch. In the first box, write what you may see at the mall. In the remaining boxes, describe things you might smell, taste, hear, or feel.

What I may see at a mall:

What I may smell at a mall:

What I may taste at a mall:

What I may hear at a mall:

What I may touch at a mall:

Science at the Park

By Kate Boehm Jerome

Summary

Parks are great places to play and relax—and great places to study science! A park provides habitats for many different animals, and the trees in the park provide oxygen. The underground tunnels of ants and earthworms help the soil. Earthworms help the soil. In a pond, frog eggs grow and change from tadpoles to frogs. Butterflies, bees, and pigeons also contribute to the ecosystem of a park. *Science at the Park* ends with tips for reducing pollution so that animals, people, and trees can continue to take advantage of these great resources.

Science Background

A park is much like an outdoor science museum. The trees in parks use carbon dioxide and produce oxygen and perform other functions in the environment—from serving as animal homes to preventing soil erosion. Animals in the park also do many important jobs that benefit the environment. Ants and earthworms improve soil quality as they move through the ground. Butterflies and bees pollinate flowers, while spiders eat insects that can bother people and damage crops. Even pigeons collect garbage and prevent weed growth. To keep parks healthy, people can do their part by cleaning up litter and recycling and reusing objects that would otherwise be headed for the trash can.

Learning Objectives

Science	Process Skills	Reading Skills	Writing Skills
• Identify trees as resources that people use and which are important to the environment • Describe the features of animals that help them survive in their environment • Explain how some animals improve soil quality • Understand the process of pollination • Illustrate the changes that some animals undergo during their life cycle • Describe ways in which people can reduce pollution	**Skill Focus** • Observing **Supporting Skills** • Organizing information • Using visuals	**Genre: Expository** **Skill Focus** • Identify main idea and details • Relate words **Supporting Skills** • Summarize • Sequence • Make generalizations	**Writing Focus** • Write a poem (descriptive) **Supporting Skills** • Prewrite • Publish writing **Speaking and Listening** • Read poems aloud

Focus on Reading

Before Reading

Activate Prior Knowledge

Read the title of the book and have students look at the picture on the cover. Ask:

> *What kind of science happens at a park?*
>
> *What animals and plants might live there?*

With students, make a list of animals and plants they might expect to read about in a book about a park. Then have students make a chart in their notebooks entitled *What I Expect to Learn*. Ask them to write things they think they will learn about these park plants and animals. Students can record facts and details about their topics as they read. They can also list facts that were new or surprising.

Preview

Lead students on a preview of the text. Point out headings, photos, captions, and features. Ask:

> *What kinds of plants and animals are discussed in this book? How do you know?*
>
> *What sentence repeats at the bottom of many pages to make the book easier to follow?*
>
> *What is one fact you can learn from the "Tree Trivia" sign?*

Set Purpose

Have students set a purpose for reading. Ask:

> *Why do you think we'll be reading this book?*

Encourage students to give reasons for their answers.

Vocabulary Strategy: Relate Words

Activity Master, Page 62

Remind students that this book is about science that "happens" at a park. Students can understand the text even better if they think about how vocabulary words are related to the topic of science in the park. Direct students to the word *litter* on page 20. Think aloud as you determine the meaning of the word and how it relates to the science at a park:

> *The sentence tells me that litter is trash that is in the wrong place. Litter can keep plants from growing at a park. If animals eat litter, they might get sick. So litter causes problems for plants and animals in a park.*

Have students use the Activity Master on page 62 to record meanings of vocabulary words. Students will work with the following vocabulary words:

antennae   pollination
arachnids   oxygen
insects

What I Expect to Learn	Facts and Details
What trees are good for	
What birds eat	
How butterflies and bees help flowers	

Correlation to National Standards

Science	Reading/Language Arts	State/Local
• Characteristics of organisms (K–4) • Life cycles of organisms (K–4) • Organisms and environments (K–4) • Properties of Earth materials (K–4) • Changes in environments (K–4)	• Read to build an understanding of Earth processes • Use text features to understand nonfiction text • Apply a wide range of strategies to comprehend and interpret texts • Use the writing process • Take notes to remember key concepts • Use written and oral language to communicate	_____ _____ _____ _____ **See Standards Chart on page 101.**

During Reading

 Read Strategically: Identify Main Idea and Details

Activity Master, Page 63

Assign each two-page spread as independent reading. As they read, students can use the Activity Master on page 63 to list the main idea and the details that support it in each set of pages.

Remind students that the main idea is the most important idea, and the details are facts or other pieces of information that tell more about the main idea. Students might turn each main idea into a question and then read to find details to answer it. The details they choose should tell more about the main idea.

Strategy Tip: Take notes

Students may want to take notes to help them understand the information in the text. You could have them set up an outline based on the contents page of the book. Alternatively, students could make bookmarks out of notebook paper and take notes on the bookmarks as they read. Encourage them to use their notes to review the main concepts of the book.

 Meeting Individual Needs

For specific strategies on meeting individual needs, see pages 90–95.

After Reading

Responding

Initiate a class discussion to assess reading comprehension. Ask:

Why are trees important? (See page 6 in the student book.) **(summarize)**

What are the steps in the life cycle of a frog? (See pages 12–13.) **(sequence)**

What effect does pollination by bees and butterflies have on flowers? (See pages 14–15.) **(identify cause-and-effect relationships)**

In general, do most animals in a park help the park or hurt it? (Answers will vary.) **(make generalizations)**

How do pigeons help parks? (See page 18.) **(summarize)**

 Writing and Research: Write a Poem

Activity Master, Page 64

Ask students to close their eyes and imagine themselves at a park. It could be a park they have visited or one they have learned about through research. You might begin by showing pictures of parks to students to prompt their thinking. Ask students to picture in their minds what they can see, hear, smell, taste, and touch at a park. Then have students use the Activity Master on page 64 to record their thoughts. Students can use these ideas to write a poem. Remind them that the goal of a poem is to create an overall feeling or impression.

Communicating: Speaking/Listening

Read poems aloud

After writing their poems, students may want to work with partners to revise them. Partners should offer suggestions on how to write clearer images that evoke strong feelings. Invite students to practice reading their poems aloud and then have them read the poems for a small group.

Students reading aloud should

✓ speak clearly

✓ make eye contact with the audience

✓ emphasize important words

Listeners should

✓ show polite attention by making eye contact and listening quietly

✓ identify images that were particularly strong or well-written

✓ explain what the poem made them feel

Extend and Assess

Focus on Science

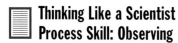 **Thinking Like a Scientist**
Process Skill: Observing

Activity Master, Page 65

Scientists make observations during scientific experiments. This means they carefully examine and then describe objects, organisms, or events. Ask students to imagine that they are scientists who have been assigned the job of making observations at the park or on the school grounds. They will be going outside to record what they observe. Each student can record his or her findings on the Activity Master on page 65. You might widen the scope of their observation by having them listen for nature sounds, such as birds chirping or mosquitoes buzzing.

Life Science: Compare Animal Habitats

Remind students that an animal's habitat is its home, the place where it lives. The habitats of several animals are pictured or discussed in *Science at the Park*. Have students prepare a poster showing at least three of these habitats. They can draw pictures or find them in magazines. They should also tell in a few words how each animal's habitat affects or is affected by its location. Have students give their posters a title.

Assessment Options

Use the following assessment options to assess understanding of *Science at the Park*.

Questions

Ask the following questions during individual conferences, or have students write the answers independently in their notebooks:

1 Give two reasons why trees are important.

2 Describe the way that birds and butterflies pollinate flowers.

3 What are the two places frogs live as they develop, and when do they live in each place?

4 Explain why litter is bad for a park, and tell two ways to prevent it.

5 Tell how earthworms, ants, and spiders are important to the health of the environment.

Assessment Activity

Students can create guidebooks for a park they have visited or read about. The guidebooks should include important facts that park visitors should know, such as types of animals in the park and where they can be found. Students can draw pictures, create maps and checklists, give tips for observing animals, and so on.

Guidebooks should

✓ give specific details about animals, plants, and special features in a park

✓ include at least one map or diagram of some feature in the park

✓ recommend several ways that visitors can enjoy the park

✓ include ideas for reducing litter at the park

Multiple-Choice Test

Use the multiple-choice test on page 112.

Cross-Curricular Connection

Social Studies

The first large city park in the United States was Central Park in New York City, designed by Frederick Law Olmsted. Other cities soon followed this model. Students can research Olmsted's work on Central Park and report on it. Possible areas to include are the design for the park, the difficulties in creating it, and Olmsted's ideas about who should use the park.

Home-School Connection

Students can discuss facts they learned from *Science at the Park* with their families. Together, they can go with their families to a park or other place where they can observe nature—even their own backyards. You might copy the Activity Master on page 65 and send it home for families to record what they see in their "natural place." Families can discuss the types of features that could be observed in more urban settings and in more rural settings.

Vocabulary: Relate Words

The words in the chart below are from *Science at the Park*. Use your glossary to write what each word means. Then write a sentence that tells what this word has to do with science in a park.

Word	Meaning	My Sentence Relating the Word to Science in a Park
antennae		
arachnids		
insects		
oxygen		
pollination		

Reading: Identify Main Idea and Details

The main idea is what a paragraph or chapter is mostly about. Details are pieces of information that tell more about a main idea. Complete the chart below, adding details and main ideas.

Pages 6–7

Main Idea: Trees have many important uses.

Details:

-
-

Pages 8–9

Main Idea:

Details:

-
-

Pages 12–13

Main Idea: Frogs go through an interesting life cycle.

Details:

-
-

Pages 14–15

Main Idea: Flowers need butterflies and bees for pollination.

Details:

-
-

Pages 16–17

Main Idea:

Details:

-
-

Pages 20–21

Main Idea: Litter causes problems at the park.

Details:

-
-

Writing: Write a Poem

Imagine a trip to a park—a park that you have visited or one you have heard about. What is it like at the park? What might you see, hear, smell, taste, and feel? Write a poem to help others imagine what this park is like.

Remember that poems do not have to rhyme but they should use words that help others imagine what you are describing. Use the space below to organize your ideas for writing. Remember to give your poem a title.

1. Write four things you might see at a park:

_____   _____

_____   _____

2. Write three things you might hear at a park:

_____   _____

_____

3. Write two things you might smell at a park:

_____   _____

4. Write one thing you might taste at a park:

_____

5. Write one activity you might do at a park:

_____

The title of my poem is _____

On a separate sheet of paper, use the ideas above to write your poem. Remember to include details that help describe the park to other people.

Thinking Like a Scientist: Observing

Visit a park or other outdoor place. Look carefully around you and write what you observe in the first box below. Your list may include flowers, insects, plants, birds, animals, or anything else from nature.

In the second box, draw a picture of at least one of the words you have written in box 1. Try to make your picture look like what you observed.

In the third box, write one fact you learned about an item you drew.

My list of what I saw at the park:

My sketches of what I saw at the park:

My fact:

© 2004 National Geographic Society

Science at the Sandy Shore

By Kate Boehm Jerome

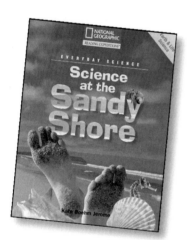

Summary

Science at the Sandy Shore takes an intriguing look at features of the ocean shore and the types of animals that live there. The book explains how sand is created and describes the difference between high and low tides. Animal adaptations and animals' basic needs are presented through discussion of creatures commonly found along the seashore. Readers learn about mollusks, two kinds of crabs, and sea stars and how these animals live and eat. Shore birds such as seagulls and pelicans are also introduced. The book points out that all of these creatures depend on the ecosystem along the shore, including the delicate sand dunes. Other interesting question include why sand dunes need protection against erosion and why the sea is salty.

Science Background

A tide is the alternating rise and fall in water level with respect to the land. It is caused primarily by the gravitational attraction of the moon on Earth.

The space between the highest and lowest tide is called the littoral zone. It is divided into three zones according to how wet or dry each gets from the tides. The first zone, the Upper Littoral, is dry most of the time. Animals here must be able to tolerate an environment with little water and a lot of exposure to air. The Middle Littoral, the center zone where tidal pools are formed, alternates between wet and dry. Creatures in the Middle Littoral must withstand hours of exposure twice a day. The Lower Littoral is underwater for most of the time. Many of the animals here also venture into deep water.

Learning Objectives

Science	Process Skills	Reading Skills	Writing Skills
• Identify animals living near the seashore • Describe the physical features of the seashore • Describe the basic needs of organisms • Relate animal behavior to environment • Define environment and explain how it affects the survival of living things	**Skill Focus** • Classifying **Supporting Skills** • Observing • Collecting data • Communicating	**Genre: Expository** **Skill Focus** • Identify facts and opinions • Use context clues **Supporting Skills** • Make generalizations • Compare and contrast • Draw conclusions • Use images	**Writing Focus** • Write a field guide entry (expository) **Supporting Skills** • Prewrite • Conduct research **Viewing** • Illustrate a field guide entry

Focus on Reading

Before Reading

Activate Prior Knowledge

Conduct an informal survey to see how many students have visited a beach. Discuss places where beaches are located, activities students have done at the beach, foods they have eaten, animals they have seen, people who work at the beach, and any other memories related to visiting the beach. Organize responses into a chart with the headings *Sights, Sounds, Tastes, Smells,* and *Feelings.* Have students copy the chart into their notebooks. After reading *Science at the Sandy Shore,* they can add information from their reading to their charts.

Preview

Explain that in this book each two-page spread explores a different but related topic. Ask:

What do you think each set of pages will be about?

Then have students look at the patterned phrase toward the bottom of each right-hand page. Invite students to read this aloud and then turn the page to finish the phrase. Do this for several spreads to show how this book is organized.

Set Purpose

Have students set a purpose for reading. Ask:

What things do you want to learn about the sandy shore?

Encourage students to give reasons for their answers.

Vocabulary Strategy: Use Context Clues

Activity Master, Page 70

Have students turn to page 7 in the student book. Point out the word *mold* in the second paragraph and have a volunteer read the sentence that contains that word. Ask:

Can you figure out what the word mold *means by reading the words and sentences before and after that word?*

Explain that using context clues—the words and sentences that come before and after an unknown word—is a good strategy for defining words. Students can use the Activity Master on page 70 to define vocabulary words, using context clues. They can then compare their definitions to the glossary definitions. Students will use the following vocabulary words:

eroding
dunes
mollusks
tide

Sights	Sounds	Tastes	Smells	Feelings
seashells	waves crashing	saltwater	fish	rough sand

Correlation to National Standards

Science	Reading/Language Arts	State/Local
• Scientific inquiry (K–4) • Characteristics of organisms (K–4) • Organisms and environments (K–4) • Science and technology (K–4) • Changes in environments (K–4)	• Read to build an understanding of seashore ecosystems • Apply a wide range of strategies to comprehend and interpret texts • Use the writing process • Conduct research • Use written and oral language to communicate • Use a variety of informational resources	_____ _____ _____ _____

See Standards Chart on page 101.

During Reading

📄 Read Strategically: Identify Facts and Opinions

Activity Master, Page 71

Assign each two-page spread as independent reading. After students read, they will use the Activity Master on page 71 to write facts and their own opinions about topics related to the seashore. Remind students that statements of fact can be proven to be true or false. Statements of opinion describe beliefs or feelings, using words such as *good*, *bad*, and *important*. Have students volunteer examples of facts and opinions before beginning the activity.

Strategy Tip: Use images to aid comprehension

Remind students that illustrations and photographs in the student book can provide information and help them to understand main ideas and details. Encourage students to refer to images in the book as they read each page, asking themselves how the illustrations help explain the text.

📄 Meeting Individual Needs

For specific strategies on meeting individual needs, see pages 90–95.

After Reading

Responding

Initiate a class discussion to assess reading comprehension. Ask:

What are some animals that live near the seashore? (See pages 9–16 in the student book.) **(summarize)**

What is similar about the way mussels and mole crabs deal with the tide? What is different? (See page 9.) **(compare and contrast)**

Why are the oceans salty? (See page 20.) **(identify cause-and-effect relationships)**

How does the way an animal uses its environment affect its ability to survive? (See pages 12, 13, 16, and 18.) **(draw conclusions)**

In general, what can you say about most animals that live along the sandy shore? (Answers will vary.) **(make generalizations)**

📄 Writing and Research: Write a Field Guide Entry

Activity Master, Page 72

Explain to students that field guides are books that contain information about plants or animals. Field guides may contain information about what an organism looks like, how large it is, how it lives, and where it can be found. Have students choose an animal that could be found on or near a sandy shore and write a field guide entry for that animal. Students can use the student book and other resources to gather information about the animal they choose. Students can use the Activity Master on page 72 to organize information for their entries.

Communicating: Viewing

Illustrate a field guide entry

Students can prepare an image to accompany their field guide entry. They can create an illustration or a diagram, or use appropriate images from magazines, to clarify their entry. Students should provide a caption with their illustration.

Images should

✓ relate to the content of the text in the field guide entry

✓ help clarify information in the entry

✓ be neatly completed

✓ include a caption

Extend and Assess

Focus on Science

 **Thinking Like a Scientist
Process Skill: Classifying**
Activity Master, Page 73

A variety of animals are pictured on the Activity Master on page 73. Students use the pictures to classify whether each animal lives mostly on land, in the air, or in the water. Then students answer questions to evaluate the physical features of the animals.

Answers: 1 *It has large flippers and a flat body.* **2** *the seagull; it has wings to fly away* **3** *It runs forward, backward, and sideways.*

Life Science: Create a Venn Diagram

Have students choose two animals from *Science at the Sandy Shore*. They can then create a Venn diagram to compare and contrast characteristics of the two animals. As shown below, students should label the left circle with one animal, the right circle with the second animal, and the area where the circles overlap with both.

**sea star and
mollusk**

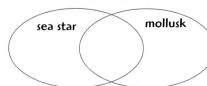

Remind students that details that apply to only one animal should be written in the part of the appropriate circle that does not overlap. Students should write details that apply to both animals in the overlapping area.

Assessment Options

Use the following assessment options to assess understanding of *Science at the Sandy Shore.*

Questions

Ask the following questions during individual conferences or ask students to write the answers independently:

1 Name four animals that live near the sandy shore. Explain one thing each animal does that helps it to survive.

2 How is sand formed?

3 What is a tide? How does it work?

4 Describe three of an animal's basic needs.

5 Why is it important to protect dunes?

Assessment Activity

Have students write a book review of *Science at the Sandy Shore*. Remind them to support all opinions with information from the book. Students should answer these questions to complete their reviews:

> *What is your favorite part of the book? Why?*
>
> *Explain three things that you learned from the book.*
>
> *Would you recommend this book to a friend? Why or why not?*

Book reviews should

✓ address each question

✓ include accurate information

✓ support opinions with details from the text

Multiple-Choice Test

Use the multiple-choice test on page 113.

Cross-Curricular Connection

Mathematics

Of all the water on Earth, 97 percent is salt water. The other 3 percent is fresh water. Discuss with students the meaning of 100 percent and percentages as parts of a whole. Have students create a circle graph colored and labeled to show the amounts of salt water and fresh water.

You may want to work with students to help them represent 3 percent on the circle graph. First, have them divide the circle into four equal parts. Then have them divide one of these parts in half. Each small segment now represents about 12 percent. Divide one of these parts in half to represent about 6 percent, then divide one of these parts in half again to represent about 3 percent.

Home-School Connection

Students can discuss the types of animals they learned about in *Science at the Sandy Shore* with their families. Together, the family can plan an imaginary trip to a beach. They can create a list of things to take with them, activities to do at the beach, and animals that they might see while they are there. Parents can identify beaches on a state or United States map to show possible destinations for the family trip.

Vocabulary: Use Context Clues

Read the sentences below. The underlined words are from *Science at the Sandy Shore*. Write the meaning of each underlined word using context clues—the words that come before and after it. Then look up the word in the glossary and write the glossary definition.

1. If that beach keeps <u>eroding</u>, soon there won't be anything left of it.

Meaning from context: _____

_____

Meaning from glossary: _____

_____

2. Without grasses in their sand, even steep <u>dunes</u> could blow away.

Meaning from context: _____

_____

Meaning from glossary: _____

_____

3. Clams are types of <u>mollusks</u>.

Meaning from context: _____

_____

Meaning from glossary: _____

_____

4. Because of the <u>tide</u>, the beach was much larger in the morning than in the afternoon.

Meaning from context: _____

_____

Meaning from glossary: _____

_____

Reading: Identify Facts and Opinions

In *Science at the Sandy Shore*, you read about the seashore and animals that live there. Use the book to find information about the topics below. Then write one fact and one opinion about each one.

Remember that a statement of fact can be proved true or false. An opinion describes feelings or beliefs about something.

Animals

Fact: _____

_____

Opinion: _____

_____

Tides

Fact: _____

_____

Opinion: _____

_____

Things to do at the shore

Fact: _____

_____

Opinion: _____

_____

Sand dunes

Fact: _____

_____

Opinion: _____

© 2004 National Geographic Society

Writing: Write a Field Guide Entry

Scientists write field guides to give information about animals. Choose an animal from *Science at the Sandy Shore* and write a field guide entry about it.

Use the student book and other resources, such as books and the Internet, to gather information about your animal. In the space below, organize the information you gather.

1. What animal will you write about? _____

2. Describe this animal's appearance. Include its usual size, color, and shape.

_____

_____

3. What are this animal's basic needs? For example, what does this animal eat? Where does it sleep?

_____

_____

4. In what places can this animal be found?

_____

_____

5. Other information to include:

_____

_____

_____

_____

On a separate sheet of paper, use the information above to write your field guide entry. Include a picture of the animal with your entry.

Thinking Like a Scientist: Classifying

The way an animal looks gives clues that can tell how it moves and where it lives. Look at the pictures. Use your book and what you already know to classify each animal based on where it spends much of its time. Write *mostly land, mostly water,* or *mostly air* on the line below the each picture.

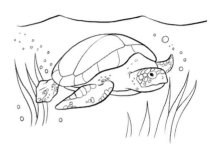

_____   _____   _____

Answer the following questions, using the pictures and what you already know about these animals.

1. What things about the loggerhead turtle's body help you know where it mostly lives?

_____

_____

2. Which animal can fly to find food? How could flight also help escape danger?

_____

_____

_____

3. How does the ghost crab move from place to place?

_____

_____

_____

Science at the Zoo

By Kate Boehm Jerome

Summary

*A*n interesting question-and-answer format guides the reader on a visit to the zoo. The reader learns about polar bear traits and habitats and about nocturnal animals and the traits that help them get around in the dark. Animal diets are also covered through the discussion of the feeding programs of several exotic creatures. Endangered species are discussed along with the question, "Where does a zoo get its animals?" Animal adaptations are presented through a discussion of giraffes' necks. Last stop is the zoo nursery, with a close look at a caretaker's job and the importance of maintaining healthy animal habitats.

Science Background

*T*he term *zoo* is short for *zoological garden*. Visitors to a zoo can observe the different animals in environments created to simulate the animals' natural habitats. Since the 1970s, there has been a shift in the purpose of the zoo—from entertainment to legitimate scientific research, education, and preservation. Behind the scenes are many zoo workers with different jobs who help to protect animals and keep them healthy. These jobs include the director, the curator, veterinarians, researchers, technicians, and keepers.

Zoos have a long history that can be traced to China—as far back as 1300 B.C. New York's Central Park Zoo, established in 1864, and the Philadelphia Zoo, established in 1874, are the oldest zoos in the United States.

Learning Objectives

Science	Process Skills	Reading Skills	Writing Skills
• Develop good explanations based on evidence from observations • Describe the basic needs of organisms • Relate animal behavior to habitat • Explain how working in a team contributes to the protection of animals	**Skill Focus** • Creating a graph **Supporting Skills** • Communicating • Observing • Collecting data	**Genre: Expository** **Skill Focus** • Make generalizations • Use sensory words **Supporting Skills** • Summarize • Compare and contrast • Draw conclusions • Reread	**Writing Focus** • Write "wonder" questions (expository) **Supporting Skills** • Use the writing process • Conduct research **Speaking and Listening** • Read questions and answers

Focus on Reading

Before Reading

Activate Prior Knowledge

Have each student write the name of his or her favorite animal on a piece of paper. Then have each student create a concept web on the reverse side of the paper that includes information about this animal. Webs can include details about what the animal eats, where the animal lives, and how the animal looks.

Have students exchange papers with a partner and try to identify the animal by reviewing the clues in the web. After they read *Science at the Zoo*, students can return to their own webs to add any new information.

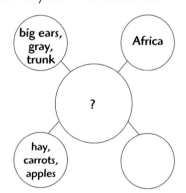

Preview

Give students time to look through the book, paying attention to headings, photos, and captions. Ask:

> *Looking at the photographs, what animals do you think will be included in this book?*

> *What information is given in the captions?*

Read pages 4 and 5 as a class. Point out the question and the lead-in to the next two pages. Explain to students that the entire book follows this format.

Set Purpose

Have students set a purpose for reading. Ask:

> *What do you want to learn about zoos from reading this book?*

Encourage students to give reasons for their answers.

 Vocabulary Strategy: Use Sensory Words

Activity Master, Page 78

Write the following description on the board and read it aloud to the class.

> *Bats have a very good sense of hearing. These animals make high-pitched sounds. The bat's large ears can pick up these sounds as they bounce off objects.*

Have students identify words from the text that apply to the senses—hearing, tasting, smelling, seeing, or feeling. *(high-pitched, large ears)* On the Activity Master on page 78, students define each vocabulary word. Then they write sensory words that relate to each word and a sentence using some of their sensory words. Students will use the following vocabulary words:

conservation
endangered species
habitat
nocturnal

Correlation to National Standards

Science	Reading/Language Arts	State/Local
• Scientific inquiry (K–4) • Characteristics of organisms (K–4) • Organisms and environments (K–4) • Science and technology (K–4) • Changes in environments (K–4)	• Read to build an understanding of zoo animals and their needs • Apply a wide range of strategies to comprehend and interpret texts • Use the writing process • Conduct research • Use written and oral language to communicate • Use a variety of informational resources	

See Standards Chart on page 101.

During Reading

Read Strategically: Make Generalizations

Activity Master, Page 79

Assign each two-page spread of the book as independent reading. As students read, they should make generalizations about information presented in the text. Students can then use the Activity Master on page 79 to write examples supporting each generalization.

Remind students that a generalization is a rule that applies to many examples. Encourage students to look for words, such as *most, many, some, generally,* and *few.*

Strategy Tip: Reread

Each section in *Science at the Zoo* is organized around an opening question that introduces a main topic. If students need help understanding these main topics, encourage them to reread a section to find information that addresses the opening question.

Meeting Individual Needs

For specific strategies on meeting individual needs, see pages 90–95.

After Reading

Responding

Initiate a class discussion to assess reading comprehension. Ask:

What allows bats to find food at night? (See page 8 in the student book.) **(identify cause-and-effect relationships)**

What is similar about the way elephants and koalas eat? What is different? (See pages 10–11.) **(compare and contrast)**

What are some ways zoos provide enrichment for their animals? (See pages 7 and 14.) **(summarize)**

Are zoos good places for animals? Explain why you think as you do. (Answers will vary.) **(make judgments)**

Is Shi Shi, the giant panda, doing well in his habitat at the San Diego Zoo? How do you know? (See pages 12–13.) **(draw conclusions)**

Writing and Research: Write "Wonder" Questions

Activity Master, Page 80

Mention that students have probably learned many interesting facts from *Science at the Zoo.* Tell them they are now going to have an opportunity to find out more about zoos and zoo animals. They will write questions about zoo-related matters that they wonder about. Students can use the Activity Master on page 80 to help them generate questions. Then they will choose one question to research, and write a paragraph about what they have learned.

Communicating: Speaking/Listening

Read questions and answers
Students can read their questions and the paragraphs they wrote to answer them to a small group of classmates.

Students reading aloud should

✓ read both the question and the answer

✓ read loudly and clearly

✓ read with appropriate emphasis

Listeners should

✓ pay attention to the reader

✓ listen to see whether the reader actually answered the question he or she posed

✓ ask questions to clarify ideas

Extend and Assess

Focus on Science

📋 Thinking Like a Scientist
Process Skill: Creating a Graph
Activity Master, Page 81

The weights of five animals from *Science at the Zoo* are listed on the Activity Master on page 81. Students use this information to create and label a bar graph. They then answer questions, using information on the graph.

Answers: 1 *Answers will vary.*
2 *hippopotamus* **3** *750 kg*
4 *hippopotamus, polar bear, gorilla*

Life Science: Simple Chart

Using topics from the student book, have each student create a simple chart based on a favorite animal in the book. Have students copy the chart shown below into their notebooks and complete it either independently or with a partner. Students may complete the chart as shown or they may want to choose their own three topics. Encourage students to use additional resources.

Assessment Options

Use the following assessment options to assess understanding of *Science at the Zoo.*

Questions

Ask the following questions during individual conferences or ask students to write the answers independently in their notebooks:

1 Name two ways that zoos can make polar bear habitats as natural as possible.

2 Identify three of an animal's basic needs.

3 Explain why giraffes have long necks.

4 What are some ways that zoo workers try to make animals' lives interesting?

5 Explain two ways that zoos help animals survive.

Assessment Activity

Have each student create an advertisement for a job at the local zoo. Ads can include a list of duties the zoo worker will have and explain the necessary qualifications for the job. Students may also include reasons people would want to work in a zoo. Students should include at least one illustration of the animal or the workspace for the position.

Advertisements should

✓ describe the kind of work the employee will do

✓ tell what qualities a good zoo worker should have

✓ include photographs or drawings that highlight animals, responsibilities, or workspace

Multiple-Choice Test

Use the multiple-choice test on page 114.

Cross-Curricular Connection

Social Studies

On the board, create a list of zoo animals students have read about. Have students choose five animals and research where each is from. Students should also find information about the natural habitat of the animal, its diet, and the climate in which it lives. On a classroom map or a world map, help students identify the home of each animal and provide brief notes about the environment.

Home-School Connection

With their families, students can discuss the types of animals they learned about in *Science at the Zoo*, as well as zoos' efforts to protect wildlife. Together, the family can talk about the importance of conservation and how it affects people and animals. Families may also identify conservation programs, such as recycling or animal protection initiatives, taking place in their community.

Polar Bears	
Home and habitat	
Diet	
Adaptations	

Vocabulary: Use Sensory Words

The words below are from *Science at the Zoo.* Use the book and its glossary to write the definition of each word. Then list sensory words that describe the word by telling what you might see, feel, taste, smell, or hear. Finally, write a sentence about the word using some of your sensory words.

conservation

Meaning:

Sensory words:

My sentence:

habitat

Meaning:

Sensory words:

My sentence:

endangered species

Meaning:

Sensory words:

My sentence:

nocturnal

Meaning:

Sensory words:

My sentence:

Reading: Make Generalizations

A generalization is a rule that applies to many examples. Read each generalization about topics in *Science at the Zoo*. For each generalization, find examples in the book that support it. Remember that generalizations use words like *most, many, some, generally,* and *few.*

Generalization: A zoo has many different kinds of animals.

Examples:

-
-
-

Generalization: Animals find food in many different ways.

Examples:

-
-
-

Generalization: Habitats are generally different for different animals.

Examples:

-
-
-

Generalization: Most zoo animals enjoy activities for enrichment.

Examples:

-
-
-

Writing: Write "Wonder" Questions

Are there more things you want to know about zoo animals? Use the questions below to help you write "I wonder" questions. When you finish, choose one of your questions and find information to answer it. You can use a book, magazine, or the Internet. Then write a paragraph to answer your question.

1. What is a question I have about the way a certain animal looks?

I wonder _____

_____

2. What is a question I have about the habitat a certain animal needs to be comfortable?

I wonder _____

_____

3. What is a question I have about a certain animal's diet?

I wonder _____

_____

4. What is a question I have about zookeepers?

I wonder _____

_____

5. What is another question I have about zoos or zoo animals?

I wonder _____

_____

Put a star next to the question you are going to answer. On another sheet of paper, write your paragraph to answer the question.

Thinking Like a Scientist: Creating a Graph

Animals come in all shapes and sizes. The chart below tells the average weights in kilograms for adult males for five of the animals in *Science at the Zoo*. Use this information to create a bar graph. Draw bars to show the weight of each animal. Then label each bar. The first one is done for you.

Animal	Weight
polar bear	450 kg
gorilla	200 kg
giant panda	140 kg
hippopotamus	1,400 kg
giraffe	1,200 kg

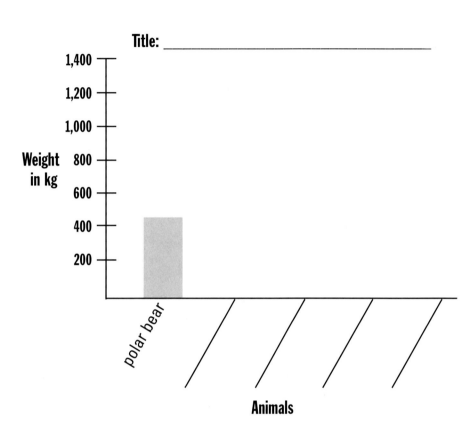

Now answer the following questions, using your graph.

1. What is a good title for your graph? Write it on the line provided.

2. Which animal is the heaviest? _____

3. How much heavier is a giraffe than a polar bear? _____

4. Put the polar bear, gorilla, and hippopotamus in order from heaviest to lightest.

_____

_____

_____

© 2004 National Geographic Society

The Science of You

By Kate Boehm Jerome

Summary

The Science of You answers some of the questions about the human body that may pop into readers' heads. The book discusses why haircuts don't hurt and what causes blinking and tears. Motion sickness and the reasons why people sweat are described, along with the mysteries of hiccups and sleep. The book ends with an explanation of heartbeats and saliva. The question-and-answer format piques reader interest and keeps the discussion lively.

Science Background

The human body has many interesting structures and functions. We often don't think about such actions as blinking and sweating, but these responses are part of an interesting series of cause-and-effect events that take place in our bodies every day. Scientists know a lot about the human body, but there is still a lot to learn. Even some common activities such as sleeping and eating are still being investigated and are the topics of a vast amount of scientific research.

Learning Objectives

Science

- Identify structures in the human body and how they function
- Describe processes that take place within the human body
- Describe how external stimuli can affect the human body
- Explain ways that people can keep their bodies healthy
- Identify ways that technology has helped scientists learn about the human body

Process Skills

Skill Focus
- Collecting data

Supporting Skills
- Observing
- Measuring

Reading Skills

Genre: Expository

Skill Focus
- Identify cause-and-effect relationships
- Use specialized words

Supporting Skills
- Make judgments
- Identify main idea and details
- Draw conclusions

Writing Skills

Writing Focus
- Write steps in a process (expository)

Supporting Skills
- Prewrite
- Conduct research

Viewing
- Create a diagram

Focus on Reading

Before Reading

Activate Prior Knowledge

Have students look at their hands, head, eyes, and mouth, using a mirror if possible. Have them list observations about each body part and tell things that they know about each one. Begin a K-W-L chart on the board, writing students' responses in the K (What We Know) column. Then have students tell what they want to learn about these parts of the body, listing responses in the second column of the chart (What We Want to Know). Have students copy the chart into a notebook. They can complete the third column (What We Learned) after reading *The Science of You*.

Preview

Give students time to look through the book, paying attention to headings, subheads, and photos. When they have finished previewing the reading, ask:

Looking at the photographs, can you tell who or what is the subject of this book?

After reading the contents page, what can you tell about the topics in the book?

Set Purpose

Ask students whether this book reminds them of other books they have read. Have students set a purpose for reading. Ask:

What information do you want to learn about how our bodies work?

Encourage students to give reasons for their answers.

Vocabulary Strategy: Use Specialized Words

Activity Master, Page 86

Explain to students that some words may be used to describe a certain topic. These words can be grouped because their meanings are related in some way. The words on the Activity Master on page 86 are specialized in that all have something to do with the human body. Have students use the glossary to define each word. Students then write one sentence to explain how each word relates to the human body. Students will use these vocabulary words:

diaphragm
follicle
salivary glands
sweat glands
tears

The Science of You

What I Know	What I Want to Know	What I Learned

Correlation to National Standards

Science	Reading/Language Arts	State/Local
• Characteristics of organisms (K–4) • Organisms and environments (K–4) • Science and technology (K–4) • Personal health (K–4)	• Read to build an understanding of human body structures and functions • Apply a wide range of strategies to comprehend and interpret texts • Use the writing process • Conduct research • Use written and oral language to communicate • Use a variety of informational resources	_____ _____ _____ _____ **See Standards Chart on page 101.**

During Reading

 Read Strategically: Identify Cause-and-Effect Relationships

Activity Master, Page 87

As students read, have them use the Activity Master on page 87 to focus on the cause-and-effect relationships between certain environmental stimuli and how the human body reacts. Remind students that an effect is what happens and the cause is why it happens.

Strategy Tip: Paraphrase

Suggest that students restate in their own words any passages they would like to clarify for themselves. They can paraphrase one sentence or an entire paragraph. Explain that paraphrasing requires students to identify important ideas and summarize them.

Meeting Individual Needs

For specific strategies on meeting individual needs, see pages 90–95.

After Reading

Responding

Initiate a class discussion to assess reading comprehension. Ask:

When you are in a roller coaster or on a bumpy car ride, what besides the motion may make you feel sick? (See pages 10–11 in the student book.) **(draw conclusions)**

What are possible causes for hiccups and blinking? (See pages 8–9 and 14–15.) **(recognize cause-and-effect relationships)**

What happens during REM sleep? (See pages 16–17.) **(summarize)**

What are some ways that the SA node in your heart regulates your heartbeat? (See pages 18–19.) **(identify main idea and details)**

Which of the body's responses that you have learned about do you find most interesting? Why? (Answers will vary.) **(make judgments)**

Writing and Research: Write Steps in a Process

Activity Master, Page 88

Explain to students that they will research and write the steps for one of the processes discussed in *The Science of You*. They can choose to explain the function of tears, why people get motion sickness, or the importance of saliva. Students should include not only what happens but also the body parts that contribute to what happens. They can use the Activity Master on page 88 to plan their list of steps. Students can get more information from the Internet and other resources.

Communicating: Viewing

Create a diagram

Have students create a diagram to illustrate the process that they wrote about. They can refer to the research they used when writing their papers. Students should show the parts of the body involved in the process and label each part properly. They should also title their diagrams.

Diagrams should

✓ show each part of the human body involved in the process

✓ use accurate names for processes and body parts

✓ include a title to summarize the diagram

Extend and Assess

Focus on Science

Thinking Like a Scientist
Process Skill: Collecting Data
Activity Master, Page 89

Students have learned about heart rate and about factors that change it. Using the Activity Master on page 89, students change their heart rate through activity, record it, and compare it to a resting rate. Then students answer questions about resting and active heart rate. To do this activity, watches or a clock with a second hand should be available.

Answers: 1 *about 35 beats in 30 seconds* **2** *about 70 beats in 30 seconds* **3** *about 30 to 40 beats in 30 seconds* **4** *Answers include flushed face, increased breathing, and sweating.*

Life Science: Problem-Solution Chart

Have students create a two-column problem-solution chart, listing a problem experienced by the human body in one column and one possible solution that the human body uses to correct it in the second column. (See below.) Have students use the questions at the beginning of each section of their books to help them think of problems and solutions. Students should include at least three entries in their charts.

Problem	Solution
dust in your eyes	tears produced to wash them

Assessment Options

Use the following assessment options to assess understanding of *The Science of You.*

Questions

Ask the following questions during individual conferences, or have students write the answers independently in their notebooks:

1 Name one way the environment outside the body can affect the body's reactions.

2 Name two processes of the human body described in this book, and tell how each works.

3 What are sweat glands and salivary glands, and what do they do?

4 What are some body processes that change when we are upset or nervous?

5 What are some reasons that scientists think humans sleep?

Assessment Activity

When we are scared, our bodies enter what is known as "fight or flight" mode. In this mode, the body prepares to get out of a threatening environment. Heart rate increases, and the body produces more sweat and less saliva. Discuss these processes with students. Then have them work in pairs to create a poster illustrating the relationship between environmental stimulation, heart rate, saliva, and sweat.

Students should include captions explaining what is happening to each component of the human body.

Posters should

✓ include an illustration of each part of the body involved with the environmental stimulation

✓ accurately represent how each part of the body works

✓ include captions that explain what is going on

Multiple-Choice Test
Use the multiple-choice test on page 115.

Cross-Curricular Connection

Literature
Additional information about common bodily responses can be found in Brigid Avison's *I Wonder Why I Blink and Other Questions About My Body.* Have students read it to see what answers it provides to questions they posed earlier in the lesson.

Home-School Connection

Students can discuss with their families the types of body features and functions that they learned about in *The Science of You.* The family can create other questions about the body, such as "Why do I cough and sneeze?" Together, the family can research the answers to their questions.

Vocabulary: Use Specialized Words

Some words can be used to describe specific topics. The words below are from *The Science of You*. First, use your glossary to define each word. Then write a sentence explaining what each word has to do with the human body.

1. diaphragm

Definition: _____

My sentence: _____

_____

2. follicle

Definition: _____

My sentence: _____

_____

3. salivary glands

Definition: _____

My sentence: _____

_____

4. sweat glands

Definition: _____

My sentence: _____

_____

5. tears

Definition: _____

My sentence: _____

_____

Reading: Identify Cause-and-Effect Relationships

As you read *The Science of You,* think about what causes your body to react in certain ways. Then think of the effects this has on what your body does. To find the effect of each cause in the chart, read the cause and ask, "What happened because of this?" To find what caused an effect, ask, "Why did this happen?" Write your answers in the chart. There may be more than one possible answer for each.

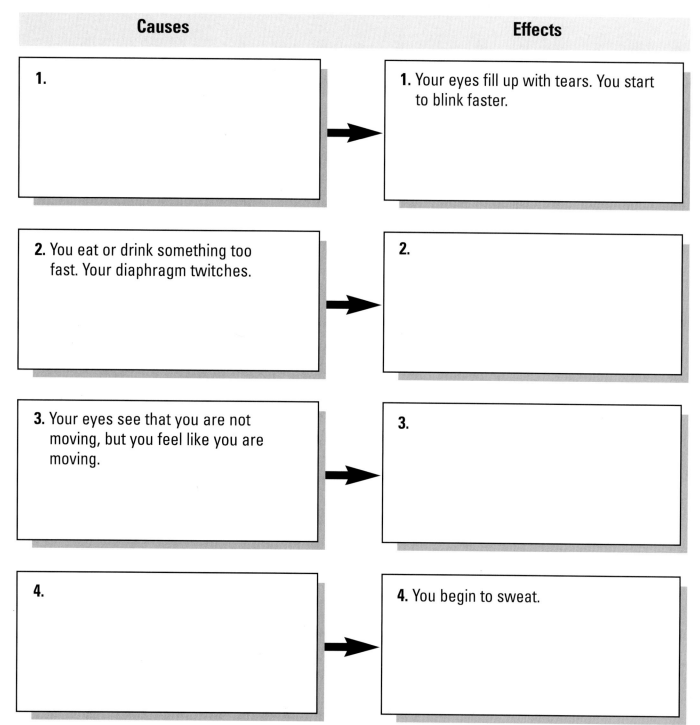

Causes

Effects

1.

1. Your eyes fill up with tears. You start to blink faster.

2. You eat or drink something too fast. Your diaphragm twitches.

2.

3. Your eyes see that you are not moving, but you feel like you are moving.

3.

4.

4. You begin to sweat.

Reading Strategies

Writing: Write Steps in a Process

Each of the body's systems involves a process and many different parts. You will research and write the steps for one of the following processes: producing tears, getting motion sickness, or producing saliva.

Use the student book and other resources, such as library books and the Internet, to gather information about the process. In the space below, organize the information you gather.

1. What process will you write about? _____

2. What parts of the body are used in the process?

_____

_____

3. How does this process help the body?

_____

_____

4. Other information to include:

_____

_____

_____

_____

5. List the steps in the process.

_____

_____

_____

_____

_____

Thinking Like a Scientist: Collecting Data

You read that your heart rate changes if you are exercising or scared. You also know that you have a heartbeat even when you are sitting very still. You can find it by placing two fingers on the inside of your wrist around the area where you would wear a watch. Do this to find a pulse.

Work with a partner to follow the directions below. Then answer each question, using the information you collect.

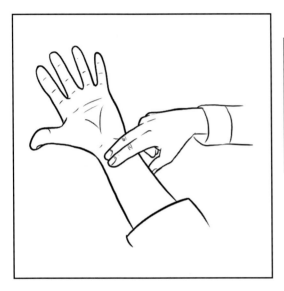

	Trial One	Trial Two
Resting Heat Rate		
Exercise Heart Rate		

1. Sit in a chair and relax for one minute. After a minute, have a partner find your pulse and count the number of beats in 30 seconds. Write this number in the chart in the box for Resting Heart Rate, Trial One. Repeat for another trial, and record the number in the Trial Two box.

2. Have a partner count for 30 seconds while you do jumping jacks or run in place. Then have a partner find your pulse and count the number of beats in 30 seconds. Write this number in the correct box above. Repeat for another trial.

3. How much faster is your pulse after 30 seconds of exercise? Explain why the pulse rate increased.

_____

_____

4. Tell two other things that happen to your body when you exercise. Did you experience these two things? Explain.

_____

_____

Science Skills

© 2004 National Geographic Society

Meeting Individual Needs

Teachers need to provide students with an education that prepares them to participate fully in the social, cultural, and economic life of the community and the country. Yet many challenges face today's classroom teachers. The student population reflects a wide diversity of cultures, languages, background experiences, learning styles, and ability levels. *Reading Expeditions* provides specific strategies that help teachers address the diverse needs of their students.

Gifted and Talented Students

Gifted and talented students are sometimes difficult to identify. These students can appear to be the most involved and creative, or they can be the most apathetic students in your classroom.

The strategies on the next page allow the classroom teacher to provide higher-level activities that benefit all students but that are particularly beneficial to gifted and talented students.

A gifted and talented student may exhibit any number of these qualities:

- Advanced cognitive ability and intellectual curiosity
- Dislike of drill and routine
- Creativity and sensitivity
- Strong motivation for self-selected projects and personal interests
- Gap between intellectual abilities and emotional, social, and physical maturity
- Unrealistic goals set either too high or too low
- Difficulty focusing attention and concentrating on finishing tasks
- Strong preference for individualized work, such as projects and independent study

When planning curriculum for gifted and talented students, keep in mind these guidelines:

- Involve students in planning, implementing, and evaluating learning tasks.
- Relate content to broad issues or themes.
- Structure work to allow for open-ended inquiry and project-based learning.
- Use outside resources, such as community members, businesses, and a variety of technologies.

Using *Reading Expeditions* with Gifted and Talented Students

Unless given unique and varied opportunities, gifted and talented students are often the ones who are most capable of learning but who will learn the least throughout a school year. It is important to assign gifted and talented students different assignments, not just more work. The academically talented student is often the one who is offered extra credit, which ultimately can mean more work and little learning for the student. Use these suggestions to adapt the teaching materials of *Reading Expeditions* for gifted and talented students.

Project-Based Learning

Involve the student in identifying projects based on the reading material—keeping choice and the student's interests as a basis for the projects. Projects may be short-term (lasting only a few days) or long-term (lasting several weeks). In designing longer projects, work with the student to outline a process that allows for checkpoints along the way. Help the student to articulate clearly what the end product will be as well as what he or she hopes to learn while doing the project.

Use the project ideas in the Writing and Research and in the Cross-Curricular Connection of the teaching notes for each book as springboards for generating ideas for book-level projects.

Involve Mentors

Invite members from the school or community to come into the classroom to work with students while they are involved in projects. These mentors can provide a different perspective on the learning tasks and offer different resources than those typically available in the school setting.

Members of the science community would be especially valuable for projects related to books in the *Everyday Science* series.

Use Contracts for Independent Study

Independent study is especially effective with some gifted and talented students. Write contracts for students so that they understand and agree to the criteria for independent study. If a student is not able to fulfill the agreement or contract, he or she will be expected to return to working with the rest of the group.

Several features in *Reading Expeditions* would work well as the basis for independent study. For example, the Find Out More feature at the end of each *Everyday Science* title suggests questions, activities, and resources for students to use to increase their understanding of the topic. Students could also read all the books in the series to gain a broad overview of science concepts. Students can share their research with the class as a multimedia presentation.

Alternate Assessment Activities

Each lesson in the teaching notes suggests an alternate assessment activity for the book. These alternate activities can provide interesting and challenging tasks that tap into the talents of gifted students. Additional assessment ideas include writing poetry, jingles or simple songs, a children's book, or a play; creating a newspaper or news broadcast, a brochure, maps or 3-D models, or an animated film or video; preparing a lesson to teach the class; developing a board or video game; producing a puppet show or play; and conducting an experiment.

Today's classrooms reflect the diverse and rich cultures of our country. Language minority students face many challenges as they acquire English while learning the core curriculum content. To adapt classroom instruction for the successful education of language minority students, there are several considerations to keep in mind.

English-language learners	To meet the needs of English-language learners, you can adapt instruction by
• Come to school with different levels of exposure to formal instruction in their native language • Bring different cultural backgrounds that will affect their own learning • Learn best when fully integrated into the school's general social and academic culture • Need to develop oral proficiency while concurrently beginning or transferring their literacy to the second language • Learn English best when it is taught through a content area	• Making instruction as comprehensible and relevant as possible • Creating a learning environment where ELL students are willing to contribute and take risks • Creating ample opportunities for ELL students to interact socially and academically with native-language speakers of English • Previewing literacy tasks with related oral language • Using only age-appropriate text that can be made comprehensible

Using *Reading Expeditions* With English-Language Learners

Reading Expeditions offers a rich selection of books that can be used to help build English-language proficiency for language minority students. This Teacher's Guide offers teaching notes for each book. The guidelines below can help you tailor the lesson to meet the needs of English-language learners.

Before Reading

Develop Vocabulary

Teach the content words that are highlighted in bold-faced type. Use these strategies to build content vocabulary.

▷ Teach the words in a meaningful context. Use the words in sentences in which the meaning and/or function of the word is important to understanding the sentence.

▷ Represent the words with visuals if possible. Use the illustrations and photographs in the book to develop understanding.

▷ Provide additional exposure to the words outside the lesson.

▷ Try to embed the words in the context of student speaking vocabulary before the words are used in literacy instruction.

▷ Maintain the same content-area standards for ELL students as for the general education population.

Activate Prior Knowledge

Use the suggested activities to tap into personal experiences and knowledge related to the book's content. Build on these connections so that students are well-grounded in the topics before reading. Use the graphic organizers suggested to make the content more tangible.

Build Background

Introduce the main ideas of the book through visuals, role-play, simulation, and hands-on activities prior to reading the book. Try a walk-through, using the illustrations to predict content.

During Reading

▷ Recognize that because students learning English have two cognitive tasks—understanding the concepts and interpreting the language—too much text impedes comprehension. Break text into manageable "chunks," using subheads as natural breaks.

▷ After reading each chunk of text, focus on the main ideas. State or write them clearly in complete sentences.

▷ Use graphic organizers to represent main ideas and related thought processes.

▷ Provide an audiocassette of the text, focus on the pictures, or use exemplary student summaries for those students who would benefit from alternate resources.

▷ Include English-language learners in instruction of higher-order thinking skills.

After Reading

▷ For **Responding,** organize discussion groups so that students fluent in English are working with English-language learners. Provide the questions included in **Responding** and allow groups to talk through the questions before initiating a class discussion.

▷ For the **Writing and Research** activity, prepare orally with methods such as an oral comparison and contrast, a retelling of a sequence, or an oral explanation of cause and effect.

▷ Provide modeling for the writing through class samples, paragraph frames, or sentence prompts that show key writing attributes, such as paragraph structure and transition words. Provide Word Banks and questions to answer.

▷ Have students pair up to share ideas orally prior to writing. ELL students can listen first and then say whatever they can, or they can listen twice.

▷ Provide alternative writing assignments for less proficient ELL students. They might tell/label/write about the photographs in the book, draw their understanding of ideas, tell or write using a graphic organizer, or use a Word Bank to fill in the omitted words in a summary.

▷ Write what the student is able to say and use the dictation as a reading source. Elaborate on the student's words by writing simple correct sentences, and read them to or with the student. Consider having a more proficient student, an aide, or a volunteer help with these adaptations.

Focus on Science

▷ Acknowledge that ELL students bring a wealth of experiences to the classroom that are valuable to all students.

▷ Recognize that students from other countries may be significantly more advanced or behind in content-area instruction received in their native countries.

▷ Use cooperative learning strategies and structures to increase student interaction.

▷ Validate the student's previous instruction through inclusion of diverse perspectives, world views, cultural bias, beliefs and values, and acknowledgment that there are cultural variations for performing common tasks. These variations can include writing structures and styles, mathematical procedures, systems of measurement, and content emphasis.

▷ Focus on the big ideas and the related thought processes.

Students with Special Needs

Students with special needs are typically unable to make satisfactory progress in the school without specific services and/or modifications made to the curriculum. Students with special needs have been diagnosed by either a medical evaluation or a team evaluation conducted at the school. These students may have more than one disability.

Some types of learning disabilities that may affect how a child learns include

- Attention (ADD, ADHD)
- Fine motor difficulties with such tasks as writing
- Speech and articulation difficulties
- Difficulty processing auditory directions and verbal commands
- Difficulty with word retrieval
- Difficulty organizing thoughts
- Emotional difficulties
- Sensory integration difficulties

Some useful classroom modifications for students with learning problems include

- Preferential seating
- Using clear, simple language
- Never assuming the student understands the vocabulary and language of school
- Pairing a student with another for peer tutoring
- Using simple one-step directions
- Repeating directions
- Making directions visually accessible
- Using visual aids, such as photographs and concrete objects
- Relating materials to real-life experiences
- Clearly stating the lesson objectives and reviewing with students what they have learned
- Continual review of what was previously learned until it is established that the student has mastered the skill

Using *Reading Expeditions* with Students with Special Needs

Reading Expeditions offers rich content and reading for all students. Students with special needs can be read to or can read books based on interesting topics that contain age-appropriate vocabulary and develop comprehension.

This Teacher's Guide offers teaching notes for each book. The guidelines that follow can help you modify the lesson to reach all students, many of whom may have special needs.

Before Reading

The suggested strategies below are especially important for students with special needs. Use these to build on prior knowledge, preview the text, and develop content vocabulary.

▷ **Activate Prior Knowledge** Use the suggested activity to assess prior knowledge and to help students make connections between the text and personal experiences.

▷ **Preview and Set Purpose** Previewing, or overviewing, is a critical first step in reading. This involves looking at chapter titles, subheads, pictures and captions, and other visual clues to help identify the main ideas. Once main ideas are identified, help students generate questions so they will read to answer specific questions.

▷ **Vocabulary Strategy** Use the vocabulary strategy to develop content knowledge based on the key words.

During Reading

▷ **Read Strategically** This section helps to focus the reading of the text on finding specific information and using comprehension strategies to navigate through the text. The graphic organizers work as study guides for reading.

▷ **Model the Strategy Tip** to introduce students to the self-monitoring and self-correcting strategies used by good readers.

▷ Assign smaller chunks of text for reading, using subheads as natural breaks. Model a three-step process for students to use.

- Read the text.
- Ask yourself what it is about.
- Put the main ideas in your own words.

After Reading

Some students with special needs benefit from modified assignments.

▷ Pair students with a working buddy who can scribe for those students who have good verbal skills but have difficulty writing/organizing language and putting it down on paper.

▷ Limit the number and length of assignments.

▷ Allow students to draw illustrations, instead of writing, to assess comprehension.

Additional Ideas

Some students with special needs need more time to fully understand a concept or master a skill. They may need to "overlearn" a skill or concept to ensure that it can be applied and remembered. Plan frequent review and reinforcement of those core skills and concepts that have wide application.

Students with special needs benefit from working with peer tutors. Explain to students the role of a tutor and tutee and then pair students so that they take turns in these roles.

Overview of Titles and Skills

Focus on Nonfiction		Focus on Science
Title	**Process Skills**	**Science Objectives**
More Science of You	• Reading a graph • Observing • Collecting data	• Identify the functions of bones • Describe how fingernails grow • Explain the role of the tongue and the nose in taste • Explain why the body reacts to mosquito bites
Science Around the House	• Observing • Inferring • Communicating	• Explain how dust can trigger an allergy • Identify examples of technology in the home • Explain how sound travels • Understand that science helps answer questions about the world
Science at the Airport	• Observing • Collecting data • Interpreting data • Communicating	• Identify ways that science and technology are used in air transportation • Explain how x-rays help keep airports safe • Identify radar as a technology used in air traffic control
Science at the Aquarium	• Creating a graph • Interpreting data • Communicating	• Recognize that many plants and animals live in water habitats • Understand that animals with different needs have different habitats • Identify structures that are unique to different ocean animals • Define adaptation
Science at the Grocery	• Classifying • Collecting data • Communicating • Inferring	• Identify examples of science and technology in a setting familiar to many students • Identify technologies that keep food fresh • Explain the use of lasers and bar codes in grocery stores

Everyday Science

Communication Skills

Reading Skills	Writing Skills	Listening, Speaking, and Viewing
• Make and check predictions • Determine word knowledge • Identify main idea and details • Summarize • Draw conclusions	• Write a newspaper article (expository) • Use the writing process • Conduct research	• Give an oral presentation
• Identify cause-and-effect relationships • Determine word knowledge • Draw conclusions • Make generalizations • Summarize	• Write a list of facts (expository) • Prewrite • Conduct research	• Read a list of facts aloud
• Identify main idea and details • Use specialized words • Summarize • Sequence • Identify cause-and-effect relationships • Make generalizations	• Write a poem (descriptive) • Prewrite • Publish writing	• Read poems aloud
• Identify main idea and details • Use context clues • Paraphrase • Compare and contrast • Summarize	• Write an adventure story (narrative) • Prewrite • Use the writing process	• Give an oral presentation
• Make generalizations • Use context clues • Identify cause-and-effect relationships • Classify • Compare and contrast • Summarize • Draw conclusions	• Write a list of facts (expository) • Conduct research • Prewrite	• Give an oral presentation

Focus on Nonfiction		Focus on Science
Title	**Process Skills**	**Science Objectives**
Science at the Mall	• Observing • Communicating • Collecting data • Inferring	• Tell how light helps you see yourself in a mirror • Explain what causes sound • Describe how radio signals are used in mall security systems • Identify ways to conserve energy
Science at the Park	• Making observations • Organizing information • Using visuals	• Identify trees as resources that people use and which are important to the environment • Describe the features of animals that help them survive in their environment • Explain how some animals improve soil quality • Understand the process of pollination • Illustrate life-cycle changes that some animals undergo • Describe ways in which people can reduce pollution
Science at the Sandy Shore	• Classifying • Observing • Collecting data • Communicating	• Identify animals living near the seashore • Describe the physical features of the seashore • Describe the basic needs of organisms • Relate animal behavior to environment • Define *environment* and explain how it affects animals' ability to survive
Science at the Zoo	• Creating a graph • Communicating • Observing • Collecting data	• Develop good explanations based on evidence from observations • Describe the basic needs of organisms • Explain how zoo workers contribute to the protection of animals • Relate animal behavior to habitat
The Science of You	• Collecting data • Observing • Measuring	• Identify structures in the human body and how they function • Describe processes that take place within the human body • Describe how external stimuli can affect the human body • Explain ways that people can keep their bodies healthy • Identify ways that technology has helped scientists learn about the human body

Everyday Science

Communication Skills

Reading Skills	Writing Skills	Listening, Speaking, and Viewing
• Draw conclusions • Relate words • Summarize • Use images to aid comprehension	• Write steps in a process • Prewrite • Conduct research	• Illustrate steps in a process
• Identify main idea and details • Relate words • Summarize • Sequence • Identify cause-and-effect relationships • Make generalizations • Take notes	• Write a poem (descriptive) • Prewrite • Publish writing	• Read poems aloud
• Distinguish fact and opinion • Use context clues • Make generalizations • Compare and contrast • Identify cause-and-effect relationships • Draw conclusions • Use images to aid comprehension	• Write a field guide entry (expository) • Prewrite • Conduct research	• Illustrate a field guide entry
• Make generalizations • Use sensory words • Summarize • Compare and contrast • Identify cause-and-effect relationships • Draw conclusions • Reread	• Write "wonder" questions (expository) • Use the writing process • Conduct research	• Read questions and answers
• Identify cause-and-effect relationships • Use specialized words • Make judgments • Identify main idea and details • Draw conclusions • Summarize • Paraphrase	• Write steps in a process (expository) • Prewrite • Conduct research	• Create a diagram

Correlation to National Standards

National Science Education Standards

STANDARDS: GRADES K–4

I. SCIENCE AS INQUIRY
Abilities necessary to do scientific inquiry
Understanding about scientific inquiry

II. PHYSICAL SCIENCE
Properties of objects and materials
Position and motion of objects
Light, heat, electricity, and magnetism

III. LIFE SCIENCE
Characteristics of organisms
Life cycles of organisms
Organisms and environments

IV. EARTH AND SPACE SCIENCE
Properties of Earth materials
Objects in the sky
Changes in the Earth and sky

V. SCIENCE AND TECHNOLOGY
Abilities of technological design
Understanding about science and technology
Abilities to distinguish between natural objects
and objects made by humans

VI. SCIENCE IN PERSONAL AND
SOCIAL PERSPECTIVES
Personal health
Characteristics and changes in populations
Types of resources
Changes in environments
Science and technology in local challenges

VII. HISTORY AND NATURE OF
SCIENCE
Science as a human endeavor

Correlation to National Science Education Standards

Science Content Standards: Grades K–4	Book Title →	More Science of You	Science Around the House	Science at the Airport	Science at the Aquarium	Science at the Grocery	Science at the Mall	Science at the Park	Science at the Sandy Shore	Science at the Zoo	The Science of You
Science as Inquiry		✓			✓		✓		✓	✓	
Physical Science											
Properties of objects and materials			✓	✓		✓	✓				
Position and motion of objects			✓	✓							
Light, heat, electricity, and magnetism						✓	✓				
Life Science											
Characteristics of organisms		✓			✓			✓	✓	✓	✓
Life cycles of organisms		✓						✓			
Organisms and environments					✓			✓	✓	✓	✓
Earth and Space Science											
Properties of Earth materials			✓					✓			
Objects in the sky											
Changes in Earth and sky			✓								
Science and Technology		✓	✓	✓	✓	✓		✓	✓	✓	✓
Science in Personal and Social Perspectives		✓	✓	✓		✓		✓	✓	✓	✓
History and Nature of Science		✓			✓		✓				

Literacy Internet Resources

Visit the *Reading Expeditions* Website

www.nationalgeographic.com/education/readingexpeds

Reading Expeditions has its own place on the National Geographic Education website. Explore the online resources that support and extend this series. This site provides a variety of options to support your instruction, including teaching materials for specific titles, information on readability levels, and correlations to national standards.

- **Comprehensive Teaching Notes and Activity Masters**

  The downloadable lesson notes for each title include a variety of teaching strategies. Additionally, for each title, you'll find printable blackline masters that develop literacy and content skills.

- **Correlation to National Standards**

  With national standards posted online, you'll be able to view how each title correlates to the science and language arts standards. *Reading Expeditions* has been developed using the National Science Education Standards and national standards from the International Reading Association and the National Council of Teachers of English.

- **Information on Readabilities**

  The online chart will help you compare the series with frequently used leveling systems such as the Lexile framework and the Fry readability formula.

- **Assessment Materials**

  The online assessment materials will include a variety of tools for measuring students' developmental progress.

Keep checking the *Reading Expeditions* site for more new resources and for updates about additional titles to come.

Just log onto **www.nationalgeographic.com/ education/readingexpeds** and see how *Reading Expeditions* continues to grow.

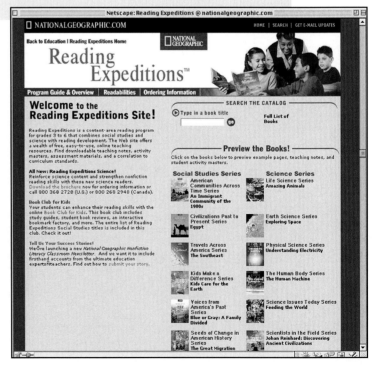

Online Resources to Extend Literacy Learning

A number of excellent websites from educational organizations and government agencies provide helpful Internet resources. The following sites may assist you in preparation for your lessons.

International Reading Association (IRA)

http://www.reading.org

As stated on their website, the mission of the IRA is to "promote high levels of literacy for all." The Web site provides a wealth of reading research materials, conference information, and articles from journals and other publications.

Reading Online

http://www.readingonline.org

This site, published by the International Reading Association, is an electronic journal for K–12 literacy educators.

Reading Is Fundamental (RIF)

http://www.rif.org

Reading Is Fundamental, Inc. (RIF), a national grassroots organization, serves young people in varied settings, including schools, community centers, and Boys and Girls Clubs. The RIF website includes information about their programs, literacy activities for children, parents, and volunteers, and literacy links for educators.

U.S. Department of Education

http://www.ed.gov

This Web site offers an ever growing collection of information about the Department, including the latest news about educational programs, policies and legislation, grant opportunities, publications, and research and statistics. The site also includes special collections of information for parents, teachers, and students.

National Institute for Literacy (NIFL)

http://www.nifl.gov

NIFL is an independent federal organization working toward the goal of having a fully literate America in the 21st century. In addition to information about programs, services, policy, and legislation, the NIFL site also offers a feature called LINCS. LINCS provides access to literacy-related information such as state and national policies and classroom practices. It also allows all users to join electronic discussion forums.

Reading Matters

http://www.nea.org/readingmatters

This site is part of the National Education Association's (NEA) website, and it offers year-round news, expert advice, classroom and home activities, reading strategies for informational texts, and resources for adults to help children improve their reading skills.

Educational Resources Information Center (ERIC)

http://www.indiana.edu/~eric_rec/

ERIC is a national information system designed to provide ready access to an extensive body of education-related literature. The database offers the world's largest source of education information, providing a variety of services and products.

Assessment Overview

Although one purpose of assessment is to measure performance so that results can be shared with parents and school administrators, the primary purpose of assessment is to gather information to inform instruction. Assessment offers valuable insights into students' learning and allows teachers to plan instruction that supports and challenges students. It deals with both the knowledge students attain and the process of learning. A variety of assessment tools is available with *Reading Expeditions*.

Discussion Questions

For each title in *Reading Expeditions*, a series of discussion questions is provided in the Teacher's Guide (See **Assessment Options: Questions**). These questions tap into students' understanding of the information in the text and invite students to use the text to make connections, draw conclusions, and make generalizations. The questions can be used in individual reading conferences, or students can write responses in their reading notebooks. In evaluating student responses, you may want to use the following rubric.

Rubric for Evaluating Responses

4	Answer addresses all parts of the question and shows sound reasoning, with appropriate examples drawn from the text to support conclusions and inferences.
3	Answer addresses most parts of the question and shows inferential thinking in filling in unstated connections. There may be some omissions or minor errors of fact.
2	Answer does not deal directly with the question but may deal with some related aspect of the question. The response reflects a literal understanding of the text but shows little inferential comprehension of the information in the text.
1	Answer shows little comprehension of the question or the text. It may be unrelated or inappropriate.

Questions

Ask the following questions during individual conferences or ask students to write the answers independently in their notebooks:

1 Name two ways that zoos can make polar bear habitats as natural as possible.

2 Identify three of an animal's basic needs.

3 Explain why giraffes have long necks.

4 What are some ways that zoo workers try to make animals' lives interesting?

5 Explain two ways that zoos help animals survive.

Teacher's Guide page 77 for
Science at the Zoo

Multiple-Choice Tests

A multiple-choice test is offered for each title in *Reading Expeditions*. The tests appear on pages 106–115 of this guide. The comprehension and vocabulary tests offer a quick assessment of basic understandings of the books. Questions in the test cover the key ideas and concept words presented in the title and provide students with practice in taking multiple-choice tests. The answer key for each test is provided on page 116.

Assessment Activity

For each title in *Reading Expeditions*, there is an Assessment Activity provided in the teaching notes (See **Assessment Options: Assessment Activity**). This activity outlines an alternative, primarily performance-based assessment option in which students can make a product or give a performance that demonstrates an understanding of the text. This alternative assessment can provide insight into how well the student understands and applies the knowledge learned from the text.

For each Assessment Activity, an evaluation checklist is provided to help measure performance against defined criteria. These checklists typically address both the content and the execution of the assessment product. Clearly defined criteria make it easier to give an objective evaluation of the activity. In addition, you may want to record anecdotal notes that give insight into such skills as problem solving and collaboration skills.

Performance-based assessments are especially useful with students for whom traditional assessment activities do not completely reflect the student's learning. These activities can tap into special skills that are often overlooked.

Assessment Activity

Students can create guidebooks for a park they have visited or read about. The guidebooks should include important facts that park visitors should know, such as types of animals in the park and where they can be found. Students can draw pictures, create maps and checklists, give tips for observing animals, and so on.

Guidebooks should

✓ give specific details about animals, plants, and special features in a park

✓ include at least one map or diagram of some feature in the park

✓ recommend several ways that visitors can enjoy the park

✓ include ideas for reducing litter at the park

Teacher's Guide page 61 for *Science at the Park*

Multiple-Choice Test

More Science of You

Circle the letter of the correct answer.

1. Bones do all of the following EXCEPT

    a. support the body.

    b. provide places for skin to attach.

    c. provide places for muscles to attach.

    d. protect inner organs.

2. Fingernails are made of

    a. hardened skin cells.

    b. bone.

    c. saliva.

    d. allergies.

3. Shivering helps your body

    a. respond to allergies.

    b. cool off.

    c. taste food.

    d. raise its temperature.

4. The part of a tooth that holds it in place is the

    a. root.

    b. crown.

    c. proboscis.

    d. nail.

5. Two parts of the body that help you taste your food are your

    a. teeth and taste buds.

    b. tongue and teeth.

    c. primary teeth and permanent teeth.

    d. taste buds and nose.

Write the letter of the correct definition next to each word or term.

_____ **6.** skeletal system

_____ **7.** proboscis

_____ **8.** reflex action

_____ **9.** taste buds

_____ **10.** contagious

a. tube-like mouthpart of some insects that is used for piercing or sucking

b. an action you don't have to think about to have happen

c. all the bones that work together in the body

d. spreading from one person to another

e. bumps that detect sweet, sour, salty, and bitter

© 2004 National Geographic Society

Name _____

Multiple-Choice Test

Science Around the House

Circle the letter of the correct answer.

1. Which of the following statements is NOT true?

a. Science is a part of our everyday lives.

b. You have to understand how a remote control works to use it.

c. Science has made many household jobs easier.

d. Bubbles in soda pop come from a gas called carbon dioxide.

2. Why does your voice sound louder and clearer in the shower?

a. Sound waves cannot travel very far there.

b. Cold water makes people louder.

c. Sound travels farther away.

d. none of the above

3. Which is an example of technology used in many people's homes?

a. smoke detector

b. vacuum cleaner

c. microwave oven

d. all of the above

4. Which of the following is NOT explained in the book?

a. how a microwave cooks food

b. why people sneeze around too much dust

c. why the batteries in smoke detectors run down

d. how soap bubbles are formed

5. Which of the following is a tool that makes small things appear larger?

a. microscope

b. candle

c. sand

d. hammer

Write the letter of the correct definition next to each word.

_____ **6.** filter

_____ **7.** microwaves

_____ **8.** sound

_____ **9.** steam

_____ **10.** allergic

a. water in the form of gas

b. causing a bodily reaction to a substance

c. a type of electrical energy used to cook food

d. an object used to catch some materials and allow others to pass through

e. a form of wave energy that is produced by vibrations

© 2004 National Geographic Society

Name _____

Multiple-Choice Test

Science at the Airport

Circle the letter of the correct answer.

1. Pictures used as signs or symbols are called

   a. line graphs.

   b. bar graphs.

   c. pictographs.

   d. photographs.

2. Bar codes on baggage allow

   a. computers to track your baggage.

   b. workers to quickly see where your bag is coming from.

   c. workers to know the weight of your luggage.

   d. radar to keep track of your bags.

3. A wind shear can

   a. keep wind very calm.

   b. help a plane land.

   c. help pilots fly safely.

   d. be dangerous for planes.

4. Because of the shape of an airplane wing

   a. air moves faster under the wing than over its top.

   b. air moves faster over the top of the wing than under it.

   c. air moves at the same speed over and under the wing.

   d. air cannot move over or under the wing.

5. People who track planes using radar are

   a. pilots.

   b. air traffic controllers.

   c. flight attendants.

   d. line people.

Complete each sentence by writing the correct word from the Word Box.

pilot	meteorologist	cockpit	radar	x-ray

6. A scientist who predicts the weather using atmospheric observations is a _____.

7. The area where the pilot and copilot sit is called the _____.

8. Security people use an _____ image to see what people have in their luggage.

9. The person trained to fly an airplane is the _____.

10. Air traffic controllers use _____ to determine the location of airplanes in flight.

© 2004 National Geographic Society

Name _____

Science at the Aquarium

Circle the letter of the correct answer.

1. Fish use this structure to sense movement.

  a. backbone
  b. blowhole
  c. lateral line
  d. adaptation

2. One way aquariums help protect animals is by

  a. caring for baby animals until they can be released into the wild.
  b. making aquarium habitats attractive.
  c. putting many different kinds of fish together.
  d. providing animals in the wild with food.

3. Two characteristics that make a whale a mammal are

  a. a lateral line and tentacles.
  b. tentacles and the ability to breathe air.
  c. living in saltwater and breathing air.
  d. breathing air and a backbone.

4. Of the following, the animal that is an invertebrate is the

  a. whale.
  b. seahorse.
  c. fish.
  d. jellyfish.

5. An important part of a seahorse habitat is

  a. fresh water.
  b. sea grasses or weeds.
  c. brightly colored fish.
  d. shrimp.

Write the letter of the correct definition next to each word.

_____ **6.** aquarist

_____ **7.** veterinarian

_____ **8.** mammals

_____ **9.** tentacles

_____ **10.** invertebrates

a. doctor who takes care of animals

b. warm-blooded animals that have backbones and breathe air

c. animals without backbones

d. person who takes care of sea creatures at an aquarium

e. long, arm-like structures of a jellyfish

© 2004 National Geographic Society

Multiple-Choice Test

Science at the Grocery

Circle the letter of the correct answer.

1. Which of the following both use light?

    a. misters and freezers

    b. scanners and sensors

    c. misters and nutrition labels

    d. scanners and misters

2. Which of the following processes causes milk to spoil?

    a. pasteurization

    b. a physical change

    c. a chemical change

    d. freezing

3. Which of the following is NOT used to make foods last longer?

    a. food labels

    b. freezing

    c. misting

    d. pasteurization

4. Which of the following is used to read a bar code?

    a. mister

    b. recycle

    c. scanner

    d. scale

5. Which of the following is a chemical change?

    a. Water freezes and changes from a liquid to a solid.

    b. Ice cream melts and changes from a solid to a liquid.

    c. Ice cream stays frozen in a freezer.

    d. Fresh milk changes to sour milk.

Write the letter of the correct definition next to each word.

_____ **6.** calorie

_____ **7.** classify

_____ **8.** nutrition

_____ **9.** recycle

_____ **10.** sensor

a. to use waste materials to make new items

b. the science of food

c. a device that reacts to light or heat

d. a unit for measuring the amount of energy in food

e. to group things based on how they are alike

© 2004 National Geographic Society

Name _____

Science at the Mall

Circle the letter of the correct answer.

1. An escalator

   a. carries people around a loop.
   b. pulls a motor up steps.
   c. uses energy to do work.
   d. has steps that stay in one place.

2. The color of a neon light depends on the

   a. kind of gas used in the glass tube.
   b. kind of solid used in the glass tube.
   c. kind of liquid used in the glass tube.
   d. shape of the glass tube.

3. For a mirror to work, light must be

   a. absorbed by its surface.
   b. reflected off its surface.
   c. moving very slowly.
   d. pass through its surface.

4. Chocolate is liquid when it has

   a. a fixed volume but not a fixed shape.
   b. no fixed shape or volume.
   c. a fixed shape but not a fixed volume.
   d. a fixed shape and volume.

5. Which of the following is TRUE?

   a. Headphones change electrical energy into sound.
   b. Sound is a form of energy.
   c. Sound is made when something vibrates back and forth quickly.
   d. all of the above

Complete each sentence by writing the correct word from the Word Box.

conserve	electricity	gas	security	solid

6. A neon light glows when electricity passes through a _____ inside a glass tube.

7. The form of energy used to operate machines and lights is _____.

8. Mall stores use _____ devices to guard against theft.

9. A hard chocolate bar is a _____ because it has a fixed shape and volume.

10. Keeping lights clean and using water-saving faucets are two ways that malls _____ energy.

© 2004 National Geographic Society

Name _____

Science at the Park

Circle the letter of the correct answer.

1. Why are trees are important?

　a. Trees can be made into products like paper.
　b. Trees hold the soil in place.
　c. Trees make much of the oxygen we breathe.
　d. all of the above

2. Which is NOT a step in the life cycle of a frog?

　a. arachnid
　b. adult frog
　c. tadpole
　d. egg

3. Which of the following animals is important for the pollination of flowers?

　a. earthworm
　b. bee
　c. frog
　d. pigeon

4. All of the following are effects of litter in the park EXCEPT

　a. litter makes the park looks pretty.
　b. animals can eat garbage and get sick.
　c. trash can keep plants from growing.
　d. it becomes very expensive to clean up the park.

5. Which of the following animals is important to the health of the environment?

　a. earthworms
　b. spiders
　c. birds
　d. all of the above

Complete each sentence by writing the correct word from the Word Box.

habitats	oxygen	arachnids	pollination	antennae

6. Plants give off a gas called _____ when they make their food.

7. Parks provide many _____ where animals can live.

8. An insect's _____ help it find its way around.

9. A plant depends on butterflies and bees to help with _____.

10. Spiders are _____, not insects.

　　　　　© 2004 National Geographic Society

Name _____

Multiple-Choice Test

Science at the Sandy Shore

Circle the letter of the correct answer.

1. All of the following help a sea star survive EXCEPT
  a. empty shells.
  b. a stomach that moves out of its mouth.
  c. arms that grow back.
  d. suction cups.

2. Which is a feature of the sandy shore?
  a. low and high tides
  b. sand dunes
  c. salt water
  d. all of the above

3. Which of the following is NOT a basic need of animals?
  a. people
  b. a place to live
  c. food
  d. water

4. All of the following are activities that animals perform to survive EXCEPT
  a. running to escape danger.
  b. singing to have fun.
  c. laying eggs.
  d. searching for food.

5. Dunes should be protected because
  a. they are good places for people to play.
  b. they are homes for sea stars.
  c. they protect the land behind them.
  d. they are food for mollusks.

Write the letter of the correct definition next to each word.

_____ **6.** tide
_____ **7.** mollusks
_____ **8.** eroding
_____ **9.** dunes
_____ **10.** burrows

  a. wearing away by the wind, water, or ice
  b. large group of animals with soft bodies
  c. daily rise and fall of the water along beaches
  d. holes
  e. mounds of sand

© 2004 National Geographic Society

Multiple-Choice Test

Science at the Zoo

Circle the letter of the correct answer.

1. Which of the following is a basic need of all animals?

   a. food

   b. shelter

   c. water

   d. all of the above

2. Polar bears

   a. prefer living in warm climates.

   b. are poor swimmers.

   c. are good hunters.

   d. eat the same amount of fat no matter where they live.

3. Most zoos don't have koalas because koalas

   a. try to climb over zoo fences.

   b. only want to eat leaves from eucalyptus trees.

   c. can't get along with other animals.

   d. none of the above

4. Animals born in zoos

   a. are always cared for by their mothers.

   b. are usually unhappy and won't eat.

   c. may be cared for in zoo nurseries.

   d. are usually set free when they are about a year old.

5. How does an animal's environment help it to survive?

   a. It provides protection.

   b. It provides enrichment.

   c. It helps keep the animal warm or cool.

   d. all of the above

Complete each sentence by writing the correct word from the Word Box.

traits	nocturnal	habitat	endangered species	conservation

6. Animals that are _____ are active at night.

7. A(n) _____ is a place where an animal lives.

8. An important way of protecting animals and their homes is through _____.

9. An animal that is nearly extinct is placed on the _____ list.

10. One of the _____ of the giraffe is its long neck.

 © 2004 National Geographic Society

Name _____

The Science of You

Circle the letter of the correct answer.

1. Which of the following is a way that the environment affects how the body responds?

   a. People feel sick when eyes and ears don't get the same messages.

   b. People sweat when it is warm.

   c. Heart rate increases when people get scared.

   d. all of the above

2. What do sweat and sleep have in common?

   a. They happen every 24 hours.

   b. They are things that the body uses to keep itself healthy.

   c. They hurt the body.

   d. They contain water.

3. Which of the following questions has NOT been answered through science?

   a. What really causes hiccups?

   b. Why do people sweat?

   c. How is saliva made?

   d. Why don't haircuts hurt?

4. What is the purpose of the SA node?

   a. to help you close your eyes

   b. to keep a regular heartbeat

   c. to produce sweat

   d. to fill your mouth with saliva

5. All of the following are structures in the human body EXCEPT

   a. follicles.

   b. tear ducts.

   c. air.

   d. the diaphragm.

Write the letter of the correct definition next to each word.

_____ **6.** follicle

_____ **7.** tears

_____ **8.** salivary glands

_____ **9.** diaphragm

_____ **10.** REM sleep

   a. found in the mouth and produce saliva

   b. a small tube in the skin from which hair grows

   c. a large, flat muscle below the lungs

   d. a period of sleep when the brain is very active

   e. drops of liquid that keep the eyes moist

© 2004 National Geographic Society

Answers to Multiple-Choice Tests • Everyday Science

More Science of You

1. b	6. c
2. a	7. a
3. d	8. b
4. a	9. e
5. d	10. d

Science Around the House

1. b	6. d
2. a	7. c
3. d	8. e
4. c	9. a
5. a	10. b

Science at the Airport

1. c	6. meteorologist
2. a	7. cockpit
3. d	8. x-ray
4. b	9. pilot
5. b	10. radar

Science at the Aquarium

1. c	6. d
2. a	7. a
3. d	8. b
4. d	9. e
5. b	10. c

Science at the Grocery

1. b	6. d
2. c	7. e
3. a	8. b
4. c	9. a
5. d	10. c

Science at the Mall

1. c	6. gas
2. a	7. electricity
3. b	8. security
4. a	9. solid
5. d	10. conserve

Science at the Park

1. d	6. oxygen
2. a	7. habitats
3. b	8. antennae
4. a	9. pollination
5. d	10. arachnids

Science at the Sandy Shore

1. a	6. c
2. d	7. b
3. a	8. a
4. b	9. e
5. c	10. d

Science at the Zoo

1. d	6. nocturnal
2. c	7. habitat
3. b	8. conservation
4. c	9. endangered species
5. d	10. traits

The Science of You

1. d	6. b
2. b	7. e
3. a	8. a
4. b	9. c
5. c	10. d

Using Portfolios and Retellings

Reading Conferences

Individual reading conferences provide an opportunity for teachers and students to assess and evaluate an individual's progress and to set goals. This is an opportunity for teachers to talk with students about their reading—what books they have read, what difficulties they might be having, what they enjoyed, what they learned or found interesting in their reading, and what goals they want to set.

While the conference may appear to be an informal discussion, the most effective conferences follow a predictable structure that the teacher and the student prepare for. Students and teachers know how to prepare for the conference, what they will talk about during the conference, and what they will do after the conference. To help students prepare for the conference, you may want to copy and distribute the checklist on page 118 or one that matches your plan for reading conferences.

Reading Portfolios

The reading portfolio is a key element of the conference. This working folder includes a variety of materials: lists of books read, writing done in response to reading, self-evaluation lists in which the student notes those things that are going well, and a list of goals for reading.

Some teachers find it helpful to have individuals keep a reading record. This is an ongoing accounting in which the student records daily reading and reflections on that reading. Each day the student records the pages read and makes notes of things to discuss in the reading conference. Many teachers find these valuable tools to learn about the student as a reader. You may wish to copy and distribute the reading record on page 119.

Retellings

Retellings can be a valuable part of the reading conference. They offer a tool for assessing a student's comprehension of an informational piece.

An unaided retelling is done by asking the student to tell you everything he or she remembers about the book. You may tell the student to assume that you have not read the book and he or she is to tell you everything about it.

An aided retelling is done by asking questions that you have prepared in advance. These may prompt the student to tell about the most important ideas, how the student reacted to the book, and whether the student can relate the book to any personal experience. See the checklist on page 120 to help evaluate retellings.

Name _____ Date _____

How to Prepare for My Reading Conference

☐ Update my reading folder

☐ Update my reading record

☐ Be ready to retell what I have read

☐ Update my list of goals

☐ Be ready to talk about things I found interesting

☐ Be ready to talk about things I learned

☐ Be ready to talk about any parts that I found hard

Notes:

_____

_____

_____

_____

_____

© 2004 National Geographic Society

Name _____ Date _____

Reading Record

Date	Author and Title	Pages Read	Notes for Reading Conference

© 2004 National Geographic Society

NATIONAL GEOGRAPHIC

READING EXPEDITIONS®

Name _____ Date _____

Title _____ Author _____

Checklist for Evaluating Retellings

The Retelling was

☐ unaided   ☐ aided

Main Ideas

☐ All the main ideas were included.

☐ Most of the main ideas were included.

☐ Some of the main ideas were included.

Supporting Details

☐ Supporting details were included and logically related to the main ideas.

☐ Supporting details were included but not related to the main ideas.

☐ Few supporting details were included.

Use of Reading Strategies

☐ Photographs and illustrations were used in understanding text.

☐ Reader made valid inferences.

☐ Reader drew logical conclusions.

☐ Reader asked important questions.

Additional Observations

_____

_____

_____

     © 2004 National Geographic Society

Using Graphic Organizers

Graphic organizers are visual representations of information. They can be used to help assess students' understanding of informational text as well as their ability to communicate information in different ways. Graphic organizers are important because they help students to comprehend, summarize, and synthesize complex ideas and information.

Nonfiction texts use a variety of organization patterns to present information. Graphic organizers are excellent tools to help examine these organization patterns as students reconstruct and process the information presented in the text. The books in *Reading Expeditions* offer an opportunity for students to learn about the various organization patterns that authors use to present information.

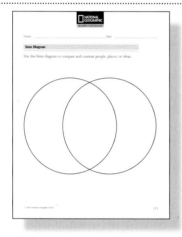

Venn Diagram
(Page 123)

A Venn diagram is useful with text that compares and contrasts information. It allows students to work with two concepts or sets of information and identify what is common and what is different.

A Venn diagram can be used with all of the *Everyday Science* titles in *Reading Expeditions*. Each of these books has information that students can compare and contrast to help them summarize the similarities and differences among features, objects, and science topics in various settings.

Main Ideas and Details
(Page 124)

The main ideas and details chart helps readers to first identify the important ideas or concepts presented in a book, chapter, or section and then find supportive details. The chart gives students practice in outlining information and in relating ideas and details.

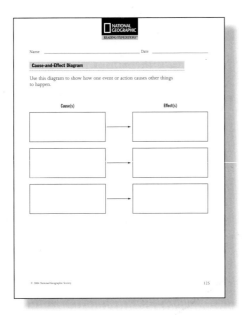

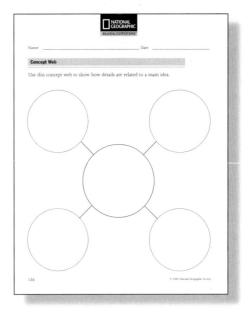

Cause-and-Effect Diagram
(Page 125)

A cause-and-effect diagram is an effective graphic representation that allows students to recognize and track relationships among events and discoveries.

While a cause-and-effect diagram can be used with many titles in *Reading Expeditions*, it is especially suited to *The Science of You* and *Science Around the House*. Students can note how different stimuli affect the human body or how evolving needs at home have led to new technologies.

Concept Web
(Page 126)

A concept web is a useful visual for showing a variety of relationships. Concept webs can show hierarchical relationships and are well-suited to show main idea and details.

Work with students to select topics within the book and then ask them to use the concept web to represent important ideas and relationships. Concept webs often show one main circle with several secondary circles as spokes off the center. You may wish to add secondary circles to the concept web provided on page 79 to reflect the content of specific titles.

Name _____ Date _____

Venn Diagram

Use this Venn diagram to compare and contrast people, places, or ideas.

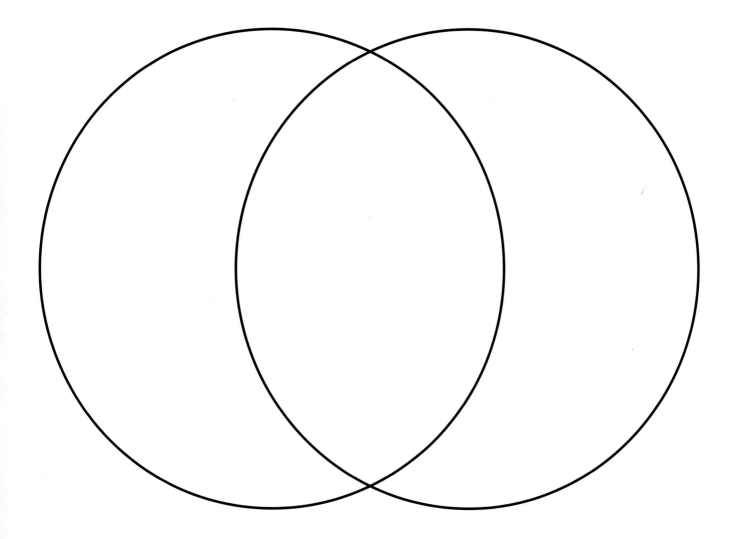

© 2004 National Geographic Society

NATIONAL GEOGRAPHIC

READING EXPEDITIONS®

Name _____ Date _____

Main Ideas and Details

Use this diagram to identify important ideas and find supporting details.

Main Idea:

Details
-
-

Main Idea:

Details
-
-

Main Idea:

Details
-
-

Main Idea:

Details
-
-

Main Idea:

Details
-
-

© 2004 National Geographic Society

Name _____ Date _____

Cause-and-Effect Diagram

Use this diagram to show how one event or action causes other things to happen.

Cause(s)   **Effect(s)**

Name _____ Date _____

Concept Web

Use this concept web to show how details are related to a main idea.

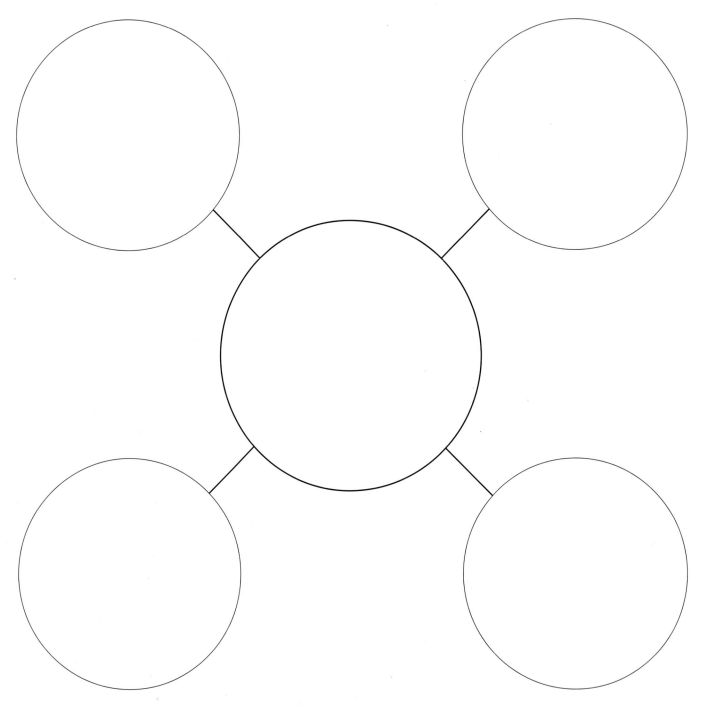

© 2004 National Geographic Society

Index

Cross-Curricular Connection

Literature 85
Mathematics 13, 69
Social Studies 21, 37, 45, 53, 61, 77

Home-School Connection

13, 21, 29, 37, 45, 53, 61, 69, 77, 85

Meeting Individual Needs

90–95

Reading Skills and Strategies

Activity Masters

Reading 15, 23, 31, 39, 47, 55, 63, 71, 79, 87
Vocabulary 14, 22, 30, 38, 46, 54, 62, 70, 78, 86

Assessment

Activities, Questions 13, 21, 29, 37, 45, 53, 61, 69, 77, 85
Answers to multiple-choice tests 116
Assessment overview 104–105
Multiple-choice tests 106–115

Communicating: Speaking/Listening/Viewing

Create a diagram 84
Give an oral presentation 12, 36, 44
Illustrate a field guide entry 68
Illustrate steps in a process 52
Read a list of facts aloud 20
Read a poem aloud 28, 60
Read questions and answers 76

Reading Skills

Activate prior knowledge . . . 11, 19, 27, 35, 43, 51, 59, 67, 75, 83
Draw conclusions 52
Identify cause-and-effect relationships 20, 84
Identify facts and opinions 68
Identify main idea and details 28, 36, 60
Make and check predictions 12
Make generalizations 44, 76
Make judgments 20, 28, 44
Preview 11, 19, 27, 35, 43, 51, 59, 67, 75, 83
Set purpose 11, 19, 27, 35, 43, 51, 59, 67, 75, 83
Use graphic organizers . . . .
. . . . . 11, 19, 21, 27, 29, 43, 45, 57, 59, 67, 69, 75, 77, 83, 85

Self-monitoring Strategies

Paraphrase 36, 84
Reread 44, 76
Self-question 12
Summarize 20
Take notes 28, 60
Use images 52, 68

Vocabulary Strategies

Determine word knowledge 14, 19
Relate words 51, 59
Use context clues 35, 43, 67
Use sensory words 75
Use specialized words 27, 83

Science Skills and Topics

Activity Masters

17, 25, 33, 41, 49

Thinking Like a Scientist

Classifying 45, 69
Collecting data 85
Creating a graph 37, 77
Observing 21, 33, 53, 61
Reading a graph 13

Writing and Research Skills

Activity Masters

16, 24, 32, 40, 48, 56, 64, 72, 80, 88

Descriptive Writing

Write a poem 20, 60

Expository Writing

Write a field guide entry 68
Write a list of facts 20, 42
Write a newspaper article 12
Write steps in a process 52, 84
Write "wonder" questions 76

Narrative Writing

Write an adventure story 36

Notes